IN THE BUSINESS
OF CHILD CARE

IN THE BUSINESS
OF <u>CHILD CARE</u>

*Employer Initiatives and
Working Women*

JUDITH D. AUERBACH

PRAEGER

New York
Westport, Connecticut
London

Library of Congress Cataloging-in-Publication Data

Auerbach, Judith D.
   In the business of child care : employer initiatives and working
women / Judith D. Auerbach.
      p.   cm.
      Bibliography: p.
      Includes index.
      ISBN 0-275-92858-6 (alk. paper)
      1. Child care services—United States.   2. Mothers—Employment—
United States.   3. Children of working mothers—United States.
I. Title.

HQ778.7.U6A94 1988
362.7'12—dc19   87-27393

Library of Congress Catalog Card Number: 87-27393

ISBN: 0-275-92858-6

First published in 1988

Praeger Publishers, One Madison Avenue, New York, NY 10010
A division of Greenwood Press, Inc.

Printed in the United States of America

The paper used in this book complies with the
Permanent Paper Standard issued by the National
Information Standards Organization (Z39.48-1984).

10 9 8 7 6 5 4 3 2

Contents

Tables

Preface

As ever increasing numbers of women with young children have entered the labor force in the 1980s, little by way of government resources has been dedicated to solving a growing child care problem. However, during the same period, an increasing number of employers have become involved in providing child care benefits and services to their employees. It is the purpose of this book to try to understand this phenomenon, and to begin to fit it into larger sociological questions about the links among gender, family, and work.

The book grew out of my interest in how the institutions of gender, family, and work intersect to create and maintain social inequality between men and women. In the course of investigating this question, it became evident to me that child care was at the core of this issue. That is, disparate but related social phenomena which are evidence of gender inequality, such as occupational segregation by sex, wage and income differentials between women and men, and the unequal division of household responsibilities, implicitly or explicitly have women's continued responsibility for child care at the center of their explanations.

But oddly, while occupational segregation, wage differentials, and the household division of labor have received a great deal of attention lately from sociologists, economists, and historians interested in gender inequality, child care itself has not. Analyses of child care have primarily been monopolized, on the one hand, by social welfare and public policy scholars who are interested in the organization and administration of child care programs, and on the other hand, by psychologists and child development experts who are interested in the effects of extra-familial child care on the development of children and their relationships with their parents. Yet, the more pressing socio-logical question about the cause and effects of the institution-alization of child care responsibility being primarily the respon-sibility of women has yet to be addressed in a comprehensive way. This book represents an attempt to move us in that direc-tion.

Fundamentally, then, this book is about the link between child care responsibility and women's status. I begin with the as-sumption that women's opportunities to achieve full economic and social equality with men are, to a great extent, limited by the fact that it is they who are considered to be responsible for child care, even when they work full-time. After discussing the factors which have made this situation produce a contemporary crisis for working women, children, and society, I focus on one response—employer-supported child care—and discuss its emergence and its significance for working women.

Let me say from the outset that I do not believe that child care should be only a women's issue. Children are members of families and of communities, and therefore, all family mem-bers—including fathers—as well as all citizens have a responsi-bility for their care. However, what is ideally true and what is actually true are two different things. No one can dispute the fact that in the United States (and elsewhere) child care contin-ues to be primarily the responsibility of women and mothers. Whether or not men and fathers *should* share in that responsi-bility is still an issue, because as a group they have not done so in any meaningful way up until now. Therefore, it is relevant to address the question of the significance of employer-sup-ported child care initiatives—or any child care initiatives for that matter—in regard to the status of women.

Employer-supported child care is still an emerging phenom-enon. While it is estimated that only about one percent of the nation's businesses are offering any type of child care benefit to their employees, this represents a much bigger number than existed ten years ago. In fact, it is difficult to obtain accurate information about the nature and extent of employer involvement, in part because there is no centralized data collection, and in part because new employers are becoming involved almost daily. Consequently, the discussion presented here of the nature and significance of employer-supported child care must be viewed as more preliminary than definitive. It is based on a reading of nearly all published material available on employer-supported child care, as well as on interview and survey data from a number of employers about their involvement or lack of involvement. Further research with many more employers and of a longitudinal nature is certainly needed in order for us to gain a clearer picture of the meaning of their child care activity for themselves, for children, for women, and for society as a whole. I hope that this book will at least provoke an interest in conducting such research, and in addressing child care itself more directly within sociology.

A number of people provided support and assistance throughout the course of writing this book, and I would like to formally thank them here.

The greatest thanks go to Mary Waters and Christine Williams—friends and colleagues who continued their intellectual and emotional support even after our diaspora from Berkeley. Their diligence in reading and re-reading material and in offering advice, criticism, motivation, and faith was unending and invaluable. Also invaluable was the support and patience of Jeffrey Averill who contributed aesthetically, as well as substantively, to this endeavor.

I was able to finish this book while participating in an NEH Summer Seminar, "American Institutions and the Development of the Family," held at the University of Michigan, Ann Arbor. I must thank the director of the seminar, Maris A. Vinovskis, as well as the other participants, who provided both motivation and distraction in appropriate proportions (not to mention some valuable comments). I would not have been able to complete this book without the early guidance and support of three other people: Troy Duster, Neil Smelser, and Arlie

Hochschild. The intellectual and personal relationships I have established with all of them over the years have been of great importance to me.

This is my chance also to extend my gratitude to the people in companies and organizations who participated in various aspects of my research. The willingness of individual employers to be interviewed and the help of various child care activists and researchers in many locations are truly appreciated.

Finally, to my friends and family, who provided me strength throughout this project with their unconditional love, goes a special heartfelt thanks. I dedicate this book to them collectively.

PART 1

SETTING THE SCENE FOR EMPLOYER-SUPPORTED CHILD CARE

Introduction

Locating Child Care
in Sociology

As ever increasing numbers of women with young children enter the labor force, child care has become a salient problem for parents attempting to balance work and family life. Not only is child care an individual family problem, however; it is also a social one because the total need and demand for services are growing but the supply lags far behind. This disparity has implications for children, parents, women, employers, and society as a whole.

Given the salience of child care in the contemporary period—especially in the lives of working women—it is surprising that it has received relatively little attention in sociological literature, including feminist literature.[1] With few exceptions, child care has not been addressed as a subject in its own right; and it has been given only brief attention in discussions of working mothers, the household division of labor, or childhood.[2]

There are different approaches to studying child care, especially as it relates to women's status, each of which could be considered sociological in some manner. First, child care can be seen as a role or a set of tasks someone—usually a mother—performs. Second, child care can be analyzed as a qualitative relationship between care giver—usually a mother—and child. Third, child care can be considered as an institutionalized arrangement, the structure and context within which child care occurs either inside or outside the family.

CHILD CARE AS A ROLE

In any society, it is important to ask who has primary responsibility for taking care of children, and why. If we assume the significance of early childhood experiences for both the developmental needs of individuals and the socialization requirements of communities, this question is paramount.

Indeed, in early sociological literature of the family, child care—actually child rearing—is discussed in the context of "role allocation" within the modern American nuclear family. Functionalist sociologists use physiological distinctions between women and men to explain why the "expressive" role—which includes the caring for and nurturance of children—is allocated to women. It is argued that a woman's natural capacity to give birth and to nurse a child make her the logical one, in an efficient division of labor, to take on this role (Blood and Wolfe 1960; Parsons and Bales 1955). Child care can thus be seen as one element of family role sets that evolve for the performance of necessary tasks both inside and outside the household (Ericksen et al. 1979).

The theme of child care as part of a set of household tasks is pursued by sociologists in different ways. First, time budget studies are used historically to measure the amount of time spent on housework, including child care, and to see if and how it has changed along with larger social changes in work and family life (Vanek 1978). Second, the nature and meaning of the housewife role to the women who occupy it has been given attention, by Lopata (1971) in the American context and by Oakley (1974a) in the British. In Oakley's study the focus is on the level of satisfaction women have with their housewife/child carer role.

Third, perhaps the greatest amount of attention has been given to examining how household tasks are divided between spouses when women work outside the home (Hertz 1986; Hoffman 1963; Moore and Sawhill 1978; Pleck 1985). The level of husbands' participation relative to wives' is measured and compared with that of husbands with nonemployed wives. Most of these studies conclude that, regardless of their employment status, wives continue to perform a majority of household tasks

(Pleck 1985). In all of these approaches (with the exception of Hertz 1986) child care is generally treated as equivalent to other household tasks.

Marxist and Marxist-feminist sociologists, too, combine child care and household tasks into an undifferentiated category, which is generally referred to as "women's unpaid domestic labor." The unique contribution of their approach, however, is (1) to consider these tasks as work and (2) to link this work that women do with the capitalist mode of production. Consequently, early Marxist-feminist discussions centered on the question of the value of unpaid domestic work in capitalist society. It was argued that, although not productive in a classical Marxist sense (that is, directly generating surplus), women's unpaid housework and child care do have value because they contribute to the maintenance of the laboring class that produces the surplus value from which capitalists profit (Dalla Costa and James 1972; Davidoff 1976; Gardiner 1976).

Later Marxist-feminist scholars have added to this analysis the question of male power (Polatnick 1974) or patriarchy (Hartmann 1981; Sokoloff 1980) and how it colludes with capitalism to relegate women to the realm of family and unpaid domestic labor. Rejecting the functionalists' physiological explanation for the allocation of tasks within and without the household, these feminist writers favor a structural one: women are *assigned* child care tasks by men who are in a position of power to do so and who wish to not do them themselves.

However, child care is still not considered in this view as a separate and qualitatively different experience from housework. Rather, it is part of the domestic role. No attention is paid to the particular nature of the child care task or to the relationship between mother/caretaker and child.

CHILD CARE AS A RELATIONSHIP

Although it is a very important question, few sociologists have attempted to study the actual relationship between care giver and child.[3] This has been left to psychologists, especially experts in child development.[4] Psychological research has focused on the perceived effects of extrafamilial child care arrangements on the development and well-being of children (and, sometimes, of their mothers). Typically, children in organized child care are compared with children taken care of by their own mothers at home to see if there are any measurable differences in social, intellectual, and emotional development and in parent (mother)-child attachment.[5] While this research has proved to be inconclusive—that is, there is no consensus that real differences exist—the questions that inform it continue to be of concern to many people (Belsky and Steinberg 1978; Scarr 1984; Silverstein 1981). Not only child psychologists but also sociologists, policy makers, and parents themselves want to know if extrafamilial—especially institutionalized—child care is detrimental or valuable to children. The assumption exists that at least it is different from maternal, at-home child care.

One sociologist who does attempt to understand the experience of early child rearing as a qualitative relationship between a child and a primary care giver in a social context is Nancy Chodorow (1978). In *The Reproduction of Mothering*, she attempts to explain from a social-psychological perspective why women in this culture mother and men do not.[6] She argues that this nurturant behavior, rather than being something that is physiologically ordained, is a product of psychological and social forces operating in this culture, a culture that has placed primary responsibility for child rearing on women. Applying object relations psychoanalytic theory, Chodorow outlines how boys and girls develop different gender identities that result from, and subsequently reproduce, this arrangement.

Simply put, in order to develop socially appropriate gender and sexual identities, boys and girls must undergo different processes in separating from their initial identification and attachment to the person who has been their primary object, their mother. Boys must experience a more severe separation, since they will grow up to be very different from their mothers. This process involves the development of their autonomous, individualist, and rational capacities. Girls, however, do not have to make such a clean break, because they will grow up to assume an identity similar to their mothers'. Consequently, during the process of their growth, they develop capacities for connectedness, nurturance, and empathy. All of this occurs in the context of a social arrangement in which women are the prime child carers—and thus the primary objects of both sexes of children's initial identification—and men are not.

Chodorow argues that the reproduction of this arrangement over the years has perpetuated strict male and female gender identities that may not have the best consequences for individuals or for society as a whole, as it thwarts the development of certain capacities within each sex, and it often creates incompatibility and miscommunication between men and women. (See also Dinnerstein 1976; Gilligan 1982; Rubin 1983 on this point.) Ultimately she suggests that if men become more involved in child rearing—by "co-parenting" with their wives—mothering would be something viewed as part of both male and female gender identities, with positive consequences for human relationships in the future.

In this perspective, then, child care is more than merely a task; it is also a relationship between parent and child that affects the development of individual personalities and social relationships. This is an important element of a sociological analysis of child care.

But the specific problem with Chodorow's work is that it does not adequately examine the structural context in which this relationship takes place. Why, for example, have men *not* become involved in child rearing? And under what circumstances would they do so, given that they have been so absent from it historically? In other words, what is the structure of social life that continues to prevent fathers from becoming primary child rearers and carers, especially now that we have psychoanalytic insights like Chodorow's?

CHILD CARE AS AN INSTITUTIONALIZED ARRANGEMENT

Thus, it is important to look at child care not merely as a set of tasks or a role to be performed, or as a psychological relationship between parents and children, but also as an institutionalized arrangement. For child care responsibility is not determined simply by physiological or psychological differences between women and men. Rather, it is an arrangement affected by the social circumstances of parents and their children. These circumstances, including employment, income, and family composition, operate together with psychological and cultural factors to determine where child care will take place and by whom it will be given. Viewing child care as an arrangement that in its many forms has become institutionalized allows us to recognize the links between families and other social institutions, and to see that child care is a public as well as a private concern.

Accordingly, some sociologists have examined the factors that influence parents' child care choices, and have found social class and mother's occupational location to be of particular significance (Angrist et al. 1976; Floge 1985; Hofferth 1979; Presser and Baldwin 1980). Others, notably Carole Joffe (1977), examine the nature of the child care profession, specifically the relationship between child care workers and families.

A different approach to understanding child care as an institutionalized arrangement is to examine the workings of governments and public agencies concerned with child care programs or policies. There is a great deal of literature on this subject, but it is important to note that the bulk of it has come from social welfare and public policy analysts, not sociologists (of politics or of organizations, for example). These accounts focus on how governments respond to the child care needs of families and individuals by providing or not providing programs and financial assistance (Adams and Winston 1980; S. Auerbach 1979; Boles 1980; Cook 1975; Kamerman and Kahn 1978, 1981; Roth 1980; Saraceno 1984; Steiner 1976).

All of these approaches to child care as an institutionalized arrangement do look at the social context in which child care takes place, but they don't, for the most part, address questions of ideology about the assignment of child care responsibilities to women (for example, even if the mother is not the one taking care of the child during the day, she—and not the father, if he is present—is still the one responsible for making alternative arrangements), or of the nature of the emotional relationship between child and care giver.

Thus, child care has been addressed variously in sociology as a role usually performed by women, a psychological and emotional relationship between care giver and child, or an institutional arrangement involving parents' public lives as workers and citizens. But none of these perspectives by itself provides an adequate sociological approach to understanding the nature of the contemporary child care crisis and responses to it, particularly as they relate to women's status.

For a truly comprehensive analysis of child care in this regard, we must understand the interplay of the basis for allocation of child care responsibility, the significance of parent-child emotional bonds, the conflict between work and family commitments—especially as it is experienced differently by gender—and the context and nature of institutional responses to child care needs. While unable to provide this comprehensive analysis, this book aims to move us closer to it.

Specifically, I attempt to identify some of the links between the allocation of child care responsibility (child care as a role) and the social context in which it is determined (child care as an institutional arrangement). While I certainly believe it is important to examine the nature and meaning of parent-child bonds (child care as a relationship), I have chosen not to focus on it here for two reasons. First, it is essentially a psychological inquiry—as in the emphasis on measuring mother-child attachment—and I am not trained to engage in it. Second, the literature that does exist is so contradictory that it remains essentially inconclusive, that is, we really do not know the precise nature of attachment and bonding between parents and children and how children's well-being is affected by different child care arrangements. Therefore, these issues, while mentioned where relevant, are not fully addressed in this book.

I have chosen to focus on employer-supported child care in order to raise the following questions: What happens to the child care role—and the ideology of mothering that sustains it—when a majority of women work outside the home? What is the effect of the increasing number of working women on the institution of child care? What kind of arrangements emerge for the care of children? What does the involvement of employers in those arrangements mean for both the role and the institution of child care? Finally, what are the implications of employers' involvement for child care and for women's status?

To answer these questions, the book proceeds as follows: Part 1 provides the background to the emergence of employer-supported child care. The conflict between the growing need for child care services and the persistent lack of them is outlined in Chapter 1. I argue that the current lack of child care services in the United States reflects the strength of ideological resistance to and political confusion about the role of extrafamilial child care. I focus on the power of the ideology of mothering that locates primary responsibility for the care of children with mothers in the privacy of their homes. This ideology contends that it is natural and necessary for mothers to care for their small children, that they should do so in their own homes, and that it is therefore inappropriate for mothers to work outside the home if it conflicts with this responsibility. It also contends that there is no place for public involvement or expenditure in such a private, family activity. Extrafamilial child care is thus resisted by many in our society because of the belief that nurturance is woman's work, that it is not something that should be compensated, and that government should not intervene in the private lives of families and family members.

This ideological resistance has been evidenced in the child care policies and programs government has sponsored since the nineteenth century. Chapter 2 offers a historical overview of the conditions under which government has become involved. I argue that child care has been provided only in circumstances of economic disadvantage or disaster. Since the nineteenth century, the focus of government programs has been on income maintenance for the poor and on control over female employment in peacetime and wartime economies. The historical overview shows how the ideology of mothering has been invoked for these purposes. The resultant stigma of government-supported child care involves welfare and poverty assumptions; it is provided only for families in which mothers, for one reason or another, are seen to have "failed" in their duties. I argue that in the current crisis, this stigma inhibits advocacy of government-supported programs and instead encourages a movement toward private, especially employer-supported, ones. I note that while government spending on child care at both the federal and the state levels has decreased since 1981, employer involvement has increased.

In Part 2, I discuss the new role of employer initiatives as a response to the child care problem. I begin with a description of employer-supported child care. Chapter 3 defines and describes various program options and the characteristics of their sponsors. Given that employer-supported child care programs are most likely to be found in expanding, highly female, sectors of the economy, the obvious question is, Can we expect an increase in programs as these sectors continue to grow? If so, what significance will this have for working women?

These questions can be approached only from knowledge of why employers become involved in child care. Chapter 4 presents the motivations and barriers to employer-supported child care as articulated by employers themselves. I begin with the reasons employers do support a program. These include the need to recruit and retain desirable employees, the desire to reduce absenteeism, tardiness, and turnover among employees; a sense of social responsibility; achieving good public relations; and responding to employee demand. Whichever of these reasons is given by employers as an explanation of their involvement in child care, all ultimately imply a motive of organizational self-interest.

Next, I discuss some of the barriers to employer-supported child care mentioned by employers who do not have a program. These barriers include cost considerations, concern about equity in employee benefits, and perceived lack of demand from employees. The last is seen to be the most significant barrier, as it illustrates the extent to which parents—especially women—are afraid to acknowledge work and family conflicts and to make their child care needs known to their employers.

Finally, with an understanding of the social-historical context and the contemporary motivations and barriers to employer-supported child care, the significance of employer-supported child care for women especially is addressed in Chapter 5. I conclude, rather optimistically, that the symbolic—if not real—significance of employer-supported child care is that it is an institutional expression of the acceptance of working mothers and of extrafamilial child care. In this way, it poses a challenge—albeit an inadvertent one—to the ideology of mothering that continues to limit opportunities for women.

NOTES

1. For example, in Stacey and Thorne's (1985) review of feminist contributions to sociology, analyses of child care are completely absent.

2. Children themselves have received very little attention in sociological literature, including works on family and gender (Ambert 1986; Thorne 1987).

3. Harrell and Ridley (1975), for example, look at how a woman's satisfaction with her two roles of mother and worker affects her behavior with her child. But in measuring only such things as the level of her engagement and playfulness, this study tells us only about a mother's behavior, not the meaning of the relationship to either her or her child.

4. See, for example, the essays in Zigler and Gordon (1982).

5. Interestingly, father-child attachment usually is not evaluated.

6. While Chodorow's definition of mothering is not clear (Gerson 1986), it can generally be understood to mean the combination of nurturant capacities and actual work directed toward the care of children.

Chapter 1

The Growing Need
for Child Care

In order to understand the meaning and significance of employer-supported child care, we must understand the circumstances that have led to its emergence. The most fundamental of these, of course, is the conflict between the absolute growth in the need for child care services of any kind and the persistent lack of these services.

In this chapter, I attempt to identify the significant factors contributing to this conflict. After reviewing demographic and cultural changes that have given rise to the greater demand for child care, I argue that the supply has not kept pace for an essentially ideological reason: Child care is still considered to be the primary responsibility of mothers at home. Specifically, I argue, ideas about mothering and about the privacy of family life that are deeply embedded in American culture and politics continue to inhibit acceptance and enhancement of extrafamilial child care.

THE NEED FOR CHILD CARE

A number of interrelated demographic and cultural factors contribute to the rising need for child care. The first such factor is women's increased labor force participation. Certainly, the tremendous increase in women entering the paid labor force is one of the most significant social changes to have occurred in the United States over the past few decades. In 1940, 27 percent of the female population 14 years old and over were in the labor force; by 1986, 55 percent of the female population 16 years old and over were working. Whereas in 1940 less than one-third of working women were married, in 1982 over half were. The most remarkable change has occurred among mothers with young children. Employment of women with preschool age children (under six years old) increased from 12 percent in 1950 to 54 percent in 1985. For women with children under age one, the increase was from 31 percent in 1976 to 48 percent in 1985 (U.S. Bureau of the Census 1986).

Fertility decisions are related to employment, and many women currently are delaying childbearing into their late twenties and early thirties because of work. This means that they will have accumulated substantial work experience and commitment to the idea of working before becoming mothers. Many, by the time they have their children, will be earning higher salaries, which may allow them to afford to pay for child care. Additionally, as delayed childbearing is associated with fewer children per woman, we can assume that a great number of mothers will return to work soon after their children's birth (O'Connell and Bloom 1987).

The second significant factor contributing to the need for child care is changes in family composition and economic status. Both the increase in out of wedlock pregnancies[1] and the doubling of the divorce rate since 1970 have led to many changes in family structure and status. Most notably, they have contributed to an increase of what are popularly referred to as "female-headed households." Indeed, female-headed households are now the fastest growing family form in the United States. They increased by 100 percent between 1970 and 1983, while husband-wife households increased by only 12 percent in the same period (Glick 1984). An increasingly larger number of children are living with only the female parent—15 percent of white children and 47 percent of black children in 1982. Sixty percent of the women heading these households were in the labor force in 1982 (U.S. Bureau of the Census 1983b).

These single, working women support their families on an average income significantly lower than that of all families. In 1983, the median income for all families with a head of household between the ages of 15 and 64 was $24,580, while for families headed by a single woman it was $11,789 (U.S. Bureau of the Census 1985b). Families maintained by women with no husband present made up 47 percent of all families below the poverty level in 1983 (U.S. Bureau of the Census 1985a).

Furthermore, experts predict that 40 percent of all current and potential marriages among young women now in their late twenties and early thirties will eventually end in divorce (Kamerman 1980). In over 90 percent of the divorce cases in which children are involved, courts award custody to mothers, and they often order fathers to provide child support. Yet recently it has become evident that a majority of fathers who have been ordered to pay default on their child support payments, either by underpayment or by no payment at all (U.S. Bureau of the Census 1982; Weitzman 1985). This situation underscores the financial precariousness of many single mothers and their children.

These factors work together to produce more working women with children to support. Unfortunately, many of them will do so under conditions of poverty unless they are given assistance to improve their economic situation through employment. Access to child care services is one such assistance. But, while the need for child care is clearly growing, the supply is not keeping pace.

THE CURRENT SUPPLY

What are parents currently doing about child care? This is a very difficult question to answer because there is no systematic, national data gathering on child care that can be considered truly reliable. Much child care is arranged informally, in an "underground" fashion, and unreported. Nevertheless, we do have some data provided by the Bureau of the Census that will be our starting point because it is the best estimate of child care arrangements available. The Bureau of the Census (1983a) reports that approximately 40 percent of working women with preschool age children arrange for care in someone else's home; 15 percent use group centers; 31 percent arrange for care in their own home; and 9 percent care for their children while at work.

The choice of arrangement is affected by the marital status, level of education, race, and occupation of the mother. For example, women living with their husbands are in general less likely to use group care (13 percent) than are other women (20 percent); black women—who are more likely to be single parents—use group care (21 percent) more than white women (14 percent); and women with any college education are more likely to use day care centers (18 percent) than are women who have not completed high school (9 percent).

It is important to emphasize that we cannot know if these figures reflect parents' true preferences or the limited availability and affordability of different child care options. All research suggests that there is an extreme shortage of child care in general, and it is likely that parents are not always able to find the arrangement they prefer. For example, a study of 846 male and female workers conducted by the Public Agenda Foundation in 1983 found that the most desirable kind of child care for working parents was a company-sponsored on-site center. Half of the parents, and nearly two-thirds of the mothers, saw this form as an excellent solution to their child care problems (reported in *Working Woman*, September 1983: 30–32). But, as I will discuss in detail later in this book, the number of employers with on-site (or near-site) child care centers is still quite low—an estimated 550 (The Conference Board 1985).

Another study determined that only 19 percent of parents who want center care for their children find openings (Clarke-Stewart 1982). And, as a final example of the absolute shortage of child care, a survey conducted in San Francisco in 1984 projected that there would be a shortage of 54,000 spaces in 1985 in that city alone. (*San Francisco Chronicle*, March 20, 1985).

Given that the optimum choice for parents in most cases might not exist, actual decisions about child care arrangements are affected by a number of interrelated factors, including cost, age of the children, and the presence of kin networks.

The cost of child care arrangements varies by city and by age of the children. Table 1.1 shows a comparison of weekly costs in four major U.S. cities. One can see from this table that infant (under age two) care is more expensive than toddler and preschool care, and that hiring a private care giver is more expensive than either center care or family day care.

Thus, it is not surprising that it appears that college educated, middle class, and professional women are more likely to use child care centers and private baby-sitters, since they can afford them, while less educated and lower income women use relatives and neighbors (Floge 1985; Hertz 1986; O'Connell and Bloom 1987). But what must be emphasized is that, in actuality, most parents do not employ a *single* type of child care arrangement. On the contrary, most use a combination of resources, so that impermanence, flexibility, and fluctuation characterize most arrangements, especially when children are very young (Floge 1985). In a four-year longitudinal study of working mothers with preschool age children in New York City, Floge (1985) found that over 50 percent of those who used child care changed their arrangement between the first and second time they were interviewed. Many of these women changed from care by a relative to a combination of relative and nonrelative care. This change was due in part to the aging of their children and to the decline in available relatives. The number of relatives available to provide child care is now declining, in part because these relatives—usually other women—are themselves seeking or holding paying jobs (O'Connell and Bloom 1987).

IMPLICATIONS

The implications of the overall shortage of child care services and the fluctuating arrangements that parents make can be assessed on at least two levels: that of women's prospects for employment and economic stability, and that of children's well-being.

The effect of unavailable, unreliable, and unaffordable child care on women's employment prospects has been documented in a few studies (Presser and Baldwin 1980; U.S. Bureau of the Census 1983a; U.S. Commission on Civil Rights 1981). Data from a 1977 Current Population Survey (reported in Presser and Baldwin 1980) and a 1982 Current Population Survey (U.S. Bureau of the Census 1983a) indicate that the unavailability of

TABLE 1.1
Weekly Costs of Child Care in Four Major Cities, January 1985

City	Family Day Care		Day Care Center		Caregiver in Child's Home
	Age	Price	Age	Price	
Boston	Under 2	$45-160	Under 2	$90-150	$260-340
	2-5	$40-160	2-5	$75-110	
St. Louis	Under 2	$45-50	Under 2	$65-80	$165 and up
	2-5	$35-40	2-5	$50-70	
Dallas	Under 2	$50-70	Under 2	$60-90	$165-200
	2-5	$50-70	2-5	$50-70	
San Francisco	Under 2	$55-90	Under 2	$90-120	$165-200
	2-5	$55-85	2-5	$65-90	

Source: Friedman (1985):7.

satisfactory child care constrains the employment of women with children under age five. In both surveys a substantial number of women not gainfully employed at the time said that if child care were available at a "reasonable cost," they would seek employment. This constraint on employment was particularly prevalent among mothers who were young, black, single, had low levels of education, and had low income. Interestingly, according to Presser and Baldwin, cost was not the significant constraining feature in the 1977 survey; reliability and the quality of child care were more so.

On a more local level, a 1986 study conducted in Philadelphia found that 26,000 parents with children under age 12 were unemployed because they could not find adequate child care (Fernandez and deGroot 1986).

The implication of this situation for potential female labor force participation is significant. In 1982, the participation of women with preschool age children could have been increased by 13 percent overall (raising it from 48 percent to 61 percent) and by 24 percent among single mothers if child care were more accessible (O'Connell and Bloom 1987). This would be beneficial not only for women and their families but also for the communities in which they live. These communities would see more jobs created—in child care services—and greater income tax revenues (Fernandez and deGroot 1986).

The lack of satisfactory and affordable child care also has clear implications for children's well-being. For it is not just the number of child care spaces that is an issue, but also the quality of programs that do exist.[2] For the majority of parents who informally arrange for child care in their own homes or in someone else's home, there are limited or no quality controls. Only a small proportion of family day care is licensed or regulated, and the requirements for such licensing vary from state to state. The most comprehensive national study of profit and nonprofit child care centers, Mary Keyserling's *Windows on Day Care* (1972), found that overall, care was less than adequate in a majority of programs. This was especially true of for-profit centers. There is no evidence that quality has been improved since the study was published.

This is not to say that there have been no efforts to improve the quality of child care programs in the United States. Scarr (1984: 185–187) reports on the activities of "a prestigious group of child-development advisors and experts from several federal agencies" to develop a set of standards for all federally subsidized child care programs. Called the Federal Interagency Day Care Requirements, these standards apply to curriculum, training of personnel, nutrition, parental education, parental participation, and staff-child ratios. But, Scarr notes, as reasonable as these standards may be, they have failed to be adopted by Congress.

In the absence of quality controls, questions inevitably arise about the safety, education, and nurturance of children in various child care programs. With the high level of publicity that surrounds reports of child abuse in child care centers, parents cannot help but be concerned about the welfare of their children, even in licensed programs.

To sum up, all research highlights the growing unavailability of desirable and affordable child care, even in the face of demographic and cultural changes that are constantly increasing the need. The question becomes, Why is this the case?

RESISTANCE TO CHILD CARE

Resistance to providing comprehensive child care occurs, I believe, on three interrelated levels: ideology, practicality, and politics. While I will discuss each level separately, it is important to keep in mind that they are inextricably linked.

Ideological Resistance

Any examination of child care in the United States must take into account a very powerful ideology about family, one that holds strong notions about privacy and responsibility for child care. Two major elements of this ideology help to explain the limited supply of extrafamilial child care: (1) the belief that nurturance is woman's work—the ideology of mothering—and (2) the belief that the family is a private institution which should be free from intervention by government or other agencies. As

I believe the first is the more fundamental basis of resistance to extrafamilial child care, I will discuss it at greater length.

The Ideology of Mothering American culture is imbued with some very strong ideas about mothering, the supposedly natural and necessary responsibilities of mothers in the rearing of their children. Aided by psychological and sociobiological theories, advocates of what has been called the "motherhood mandate"[3] contend that at least until the age of five, a child needs the nurturance of its mother at home to ensure its proper physical, emotional, psychological, and moral development (Fraiberg 1977). It is considered acceptable that a woman becomes educated, works, and is active in public life as long as she first fulfills her obligation as a "good" mother—meaning that she is instantly and constantly available to meet her child's needs. Incompatibility with other demanding roles is thus built into society's definition of a "good" mother, as her commitment to her children's care must always remain foremost. The child without this kind of "good" mother is considered deprived. In this view, extrafamilial child care is something only for "bad" mothers who are "trying to get rid of their children."

Sociologists and psychologists have contributed to the creation and maintenance of this ideology of mothering that says it is both natural and necessary for children to need their mothers and for mothers to be the caretakers of their children. The question is, of course, why they assume this is true of mothers and not of fathers.

Functionalist sociologists early approached this question out of concern with explaining role allocation in the modern nuclear family. They located the basis for role allocation between mothers and fathers in biological imperatives: Mothers take care of children because they naturally produce and feed them, and men do not (Blood and Wolfe 1960; Parsons and Bales 1955; Zelditch 1960). In their classic book *Family, Socialization and Interaction Process*, Parsons and Bales (1955) clearly articulate this perspective:

In our opinion the fundamental explanation of the allocation of roles between biological sexes lies in the fact that the bearing and early nursing of children establish a strong presumptive primacy of the relation of mother to the small child and this in turn establishes a presumption that the man, who is exempted from these biological functions, should specialize in the alternative instrumental direction.(p. 123)

Thus, almost by default, fathers are exempt from the mothering role. Parsons and Bales further argue that the "relative isolation" of the modern nuclear family—having lost extended kin networks, and relocating to the detached homes of the surburbs—focuses the responsibility of the "mother role" even more sharply on the adult woman. Their point in general is that the division of private and public responsibilities (role allocation) between males and females, based on their physiological differences, is seen to be efficient, and therefore functional for the family subsystem. It is also functional for society because it ensures the fulfillment of two imperatives for social order: that children become socialized by internalizing cultural norms (about work, family, sex, and so on), and that children develop the autonomous personalities necessary for eventually functioning as rational, gendered adult members of society.

Parsons and Bales were influenced by Freudian psychological theory, which, although begging the question of why the mother is the primary child rearer, places primacy on the mother-infant relationship. Traditional Freudian psychologists focus on such concepts as drives—natural, primal tendencies toward aggression and love—and infantile rage to emphasize the importance of the first child-object (meaning other person) relationship. The mother, since she is usually the caretaker of the child, is the primary object of its natural drives and sentiments, and in her responses to them she becomes to that child the source of all good and evil in the process of its early development. The primacy Freudians place on the first few years of a child's life has put tremendous focus on the mothering role in Western culture: We have created images of the "good" and the "bad" mother based upon our early childhood experiences of her as the one who both satisfied and frustrated our impulses.

Indeed, Freud's view that the first few years of a child's life are of ultimate significance in its subsequent development is now widely held by lay people as well as psychologists (Hewlett

1986; Scarr 1984). There is considerable evidence to support the contention that young children need a sense of security in a continuous and warm relationship with an adult in order to ensure their mental and emotional well-being. People passionately believe this adult should be the child's parent—usually its mother. This belief was first popularized by a British doctor, John Bowlby, in 1951. In a monograph for the World Health Organization titled *Maternal Care and Mental Health*, Bowlby (1952) wrote:

What is believed to be essential for mental health is that the infant and young child should experience a warm, intimate and continuous relationship with his mother (or permanent mother substitute) in which both find satisfaction and engagement. . . . A state of affairs in which the child does not have this relationship is termed "maternal deprivation". . . . Partial deprivation brings in its train acute anxiety, excessive need for love, powerful feelings of revenge and, arising from these last, guilt and depression. Complete deprivation . . . has even more far-reaching effects on character development and may entirely cripple the capacity to make relationships. (p. 11)

Bowlby's theory of maternal deprivation was based upon his observations of institutionalized children who had no mother or permanent mother substitute present. Although subsequent studies have shown that Bowlby was really studying institutionalization, and not maternal-child relationships, his work is still the basis on which extrafamilial child care is evaluated. Studies of child care to this day focus on its perceived effects on the mother-child relationship and on the socioemotional development of the child. The assumption still seems to be that the mother-child bond is primary; and child care is evaluated in relation to whether it has adverse effects on that bond.[4]

The assumptions of social and psychological theorists of maternal deprivation have contributed to the development of an ideology of mothering that confuses a set of social arrangements with beliefs about the "natural order." Of course, one cannot dispute that only women can carry, give birth to, and naturally nurse a baby. But beyond those capacities, there is no natural reason why women should bear the sole responsibility for rearing children and why their character should be judged solely by how successful they are at doing so. We must look at social, not just biological, factors that result in this arrangement.

One author who does this from what she calls a "power analysis" perspective is Margaret Polatnick (1974). In an article titled "Why Men Don't Rear Children," she argues: "The allocation of child-rearing responsibility to women . . . is no sacred fiat of nature, but a social policy which supports male domination in the society and in the family" (p. 79). Polatnick discusses child rearing as a set of tasks that offer low status and low or no pay. These tasks are assigned to women by men who don't want to do them and who wish to preserve their monopoly of the higher status and prestige that come from being a breadwinner in this society. In short, Polatnick argues that women are assigned the job of child rearing as a means of keeping male power intact: Rather than child rearing being a product of natural instinct or even of socialization, it is a measure of social control.

While many might question the conspiratorial element of Polatnick's "power analysis," I think she provides a useful, sociological way of understanding the ideology of motherhood. If one moves from the biological aspects of birth and early lactation, and looks at the nature of child rearing beyond those, one sees a series of tasks that are arranged and, in some manner, assigned. It is impossible to argue that changing diapers, clothing, feeding, talking to, and playing with a baby are instinctive to women and not to men. Rather, these are tasks that girls and women learn to do. Many new mothers, as a matter of fact, have had no prior experience with babies before the birth of their own, and have to learn how to care for them at that moment (Lopata 1971). There is no reason why men cannot learn this as easily.

But it is precisely the belief in something called maternal instinct that keeps us from viewing child rearing as a set of tasks that can be learned by either sex. It is assumed that because women have the capacity to bear children, they possess the instinct to do so and to care for those children once they are born

(Oakley 1976). But even this notion is socially constructed. Belief in maternal instinct is historically specific and relatively new (Badinter 1980). There is evidence from social historians of the family that in fact maternal *indifference* characterized mother-child relations in premodern Europe. Beliefs about the inappropriateness of breast feeding in the early eighteenth century, for example, indicate that there was no natural—or at least no emotional—compulsion on the part of mothers to nurse their babies. Other practices among the artisan and middle classes in the seventeenth and eighteenth centuries, such as swaddling, sending babies away to wet nurses, and placing young children in convents or boarding schools, suggest that parents were neglectful of and uncaring about children (Aries 1962; Badinter 1980; Shorter 1975; Stone 1979).

The change in attitude toward child rearing and the emergence of the notion of maternal instinct (or "mother love," as Badinter calls it) was a result of both structural and ideological changes beginning in the late eighteenth century. Freud's nineteenth century psychoanalytic paradigm—which solidified the mother-child bond—could have emerged only in a situation in which women were charged with the rearing of their children, their domestic responsibilities intensified by their exclusion from productive labor.

This situation has produced powerful images of the duty of mothering over the years as it has come to involve responsibility for the child's moral, intellectual, social, and psychological development (Hewlett 1986; Scarr 1984). Women performing this duty are assessed by their success or failure in carrying out these responsibilities, as measured by the child's behavior in the public world. And it is in this arrangement that the dichotomous image of the "good" mother/"bad" mother is rooted. Psychoanalytic theorists—even feminist ones—have contributed greatly to this image (Chodorow and Contratto 1982). Similarly, sociologists who take a functionalist approach perpetuate this image by locating responsibility for the success or failure of the family subsystem (and ultimately the society as a whole) with mothers. As a result of popular acceptance of these approaches, the mother-child relation is perceived to be of utmost significance, and attempts to provide alternatives to the totality of that relationship, such as extrafamilial child care, are greatly resisted by many groups in our society.

Privatism/Non-Interventionism The second—and related—element of ideological resistance to extrafamilial child care is our concern over privatism and nonintervention by government into the affairs of families. The family in American culture has long been viewed as a private realm, a haven from the rest of the world, and one ideally free from outside influence (Lasch 1977). Especially as production under capitalism has intensified, further removing a worker from the product of his or her labor, meaning and control must be found in other realms of life. The family presents itself as the one realm where this is possible, especially with regard to child rearing. The decision about how to raise a child is considered to be a private one, based upon the experience, culture, and style of parents themselves, and carried out in their own manner in their own homes (Berger and Berger 1983; Bourne 1972).

This ideology of parental determinism has limited public response to child care problems. As Sponseller and Fink (1982) argue:

There is a fundamental belief in American society that parents have the major responsibility and the right to make decisions concerning their children's welfare and future. This belief is complemented by a conviction that in a pluralistic society there are multiple correct ways to rear children. Therefore government intervention is considered legitimate and warranted only if there are deficiencies in parents' ability or will to provide adequate physical care or educational opportunities for their children. (p. 17)

Indeed, in American culture, we historically have opposed government intervention into the lives of families and family members. In particular (as we will see in the following chapter) it is assumed that government aid to families and children should exist only in the case of economic disaster or disadvantage. According to public policy analyst Gilbert Steiner (1976), nonintervention has been the basic guiding principle of family-related policy:

When politicians consider legislation affecting children generally, they do so hesitantly and reluctantly, knowing that the American social system presumes that barring economic disaster or health crises, a family should and will care for its children without public intervention. (p. 1)

This noninterventionist attitude reinforces the notion of the privatism of family life by stressing that the family is a "last bastion of privacy in an already over-regulated and overorganized society" (Steiner 1981:1).

As a result of the strength of this noninterventionist ideology, the United States is one of the few advanced industrial societies (capitalist or socialist) that does not have an identifiable family policy.[5] Child care, as well as elderly care, maternity leave, family income supports, and nutrition supplements are addressed in fragmentary policies and programs with no unifying theme. And all are approached hesitantly and with limited public commitment (Kamerman and Kahn 1978). The irony is that these policies and programs do exist. Public institutions and government programs intervene in the lives of families all the time—through the legal system, public education, taxation, and even employment policies. Nevertheless, as Grubb and Lazerson (1982:60) succinctly put it, "We continue to assert that parents raise their children privately and are wholly responsible for their successes and failures, despite the ubiquity of social institutions and public decision in the lives of children."

Practical Resistance

Many people argue that child care is not provided in any comprehensive way in the United States because it is too costly (Boles 1980). It is expensive to build and maintain child care centers, to train and pay child care workers, to cover liability expenses, or to compensate parents for reduced work hours to allow them to stay home and take care of their children. But, the question is, expensive for whom?

Currently, the burden of child care expenses rests on parents, and by all accounts that burden is great. A Carnegie Corporation study notes that day care expenses average 10 percent of gross income for the working family, making them the fourth largest expenditure after housing, food, and taxes (reported in *Business Week*, December 21, 1981). In California, for example, a two-parent family with an annual income of $24,000 must spend 26 percent of its pretax income for care for two preschool children. A single mother with a child under two years old must spend 49 percent of her income on child care (*Newsweek*, September 10, 1984).

There are significant regional differences in the cost of child care for one child in this country, as we saw in Table 1.1, resulting in a range of approximately $1,500 to $10,000 per year. The overall average expense is $3,000 per year for out-of-home child care (Friedman 1985).

The only federal program that addresses this high cost for working parents is the child care tax credit, revised as part of the federal Economic Recovery Tax Act (ERTA) of 1981. This allows families to take a credit for child care expenses on a sliding percentage scale, depending upon their income. The maximum expense against which the appropriate credit may be taken is $2,400 for one child and $4,800 for two or more. The maximum credit is 30 percent of child care expenses, and is applicable ony to families with adjusted gross incomes of $10,000 or less. Middle income families earning between $20,000 and $22,000 per year, for example, can take only a 24 percent credit. This translates into a $576 credit for one child and a $1,152 credit for two or more children. Given that the average out-of-home child care expense is $3,000, one can see that this credit does little to offset the high costs of child care for most working parents.

For nonemployed and low income parents, the situation is even worse. As part of the larger social welfare backlash we are experiencing in the 1980s,[6] public funding for child care has been cut rather than increased at both the state and federal levels. Specifically, between 1981 and 1983, Title XX of the Social Security Act—the major source of child care funding—was cut by 21 percent ($700 million), eliminating most funds earmarked for day care. In the same period, the child care staff training program of the Comprehensive Employment and Training Act was abolished, resulting in the decline of services to poor children in 32 states and the elimination of child care spending in 33 states (Blank 1984). Overall, direct federal and state spending on child care for low income families dropped 14 percent between 1981 and 1983, eliminating child care for an estimated 150,000 children (Friedman 1983a).

So it appears that at least legislators have decided that child care is too expensive for government to provide. But government spends money on many other programs more costly than child care, for example, military preparedness. Thus cost itself must be seen as an ideological issue. Governments prioritize expenditures, and it seems that planning for future potential military altercations is considered a more significant priority than taking care of the immediate needs of working parents and children. Or perhaps something else is going on. Ruth Sidel (1986) suggests that arguments about cost mask the fact that child care is still considered to be a women's and children's issue only; and since women and children have low status in our society, their concerns are not taken as seriously.

Furthermore, child care generally is not a profit-producing enterprise; in fact, many people find it problematic if it is. Children are not commodities, and profiting from their care is something that seems abhorrent to many (Suransky 1982). Thus the status of the child care profession is also a practical issue that affects the limited supply of child care. Child care is low status, low wage work. Most child care workers are women—94 percent in 1980—many of whom work only part-time. Their average pay is less than minimum wage, averaging $3.13 per hour in 1980 (O'Connell and Bloom 1987). It is estimated that family day care providers—also nearly all women—earn as little as 75 cents per hour per child. Since they are usually limited to caring for three or four children at a time, their wages, too, amount to less than the minimum (Scarr 1984).

Low status, low pay, and limited profitability do not inspire many people to enter the field of child care as either workers or entrepreneurs; and this serves to perpetuate the shortage of quality programs, even in the face of apparent, growing need.

Political Resistance

A third reason child care supply is not meeting the need in America—and one that is clearly linked to ideological and practical issues—is that there is no consensus in government and policy circles about public child care goals (S. Auerbach 1979; Beck 1982; Boles 1980). Steveanne Auerbach (1979) argues that the federal government has never taken a clear direction in its pursuit of child care policies and programs, and that a lack of cohesion with regard to premises and goals characterized its inability to extend public involvement in the 1960s and 1970s, when other social programs were expanded. (A detailed historical review of child care policies and programs follows in the next chapter.) In the 1980s, there remains no clear set of values to provide a framework in which child care policy and services can be developed.

This lack of policy framework may be due in great part to the lack of consensus within the child care community itself. There is no agreement among activists who lobby and advise policy makers about what is desirable and preferable in child care (Beck 1982; Boles 1980). In fact, Janet Boles (1980) has identified eight separate goals expressed by different advocates of child care: (1) to benefit the child; (2) to benefit the mother; (3) to employ all mothers; (4) to force welfare recipients to work; (5) to promote basic social change; (6) to change family structure; (7) to redefine child care as a social responsibility; (8) to create jobs. Clearly, each of these goals could require different policy action and program design. This divergence in fundamental goals among child care advocates mirrors divergence among lay citizens, and one can see how it might contribute to the stalemate that characterizes public policy regarding child care.

CONCLUSION

The notion that nurturance is woman's work, the belief that government should not intervene in family life, the assertion that public child care is too expensive to provide, and the level of disagreement about the goals of child care among policy makers and citizens are interrelated elements that have prevented public commitment to child care and contribute to the current contradiction between the growing need for child care and the persistent lack of supply. While I have categorized the levels of resistance into three—ideology, practicality, and politics—I believe that all of them fundamentally are ideological.

American culture and ideology generally assume that the family is a private institution and that within it reside the natural resources for caring for children. There is no consideration of paying a wage to mothers who perform child rearing tasks in their homes—and child care workers who do it elsewhere are paid a paltry wage—because child care is not seen as a set of tasks. Rather, child care is believed to be a natural and necessary component of being a mother, something that emanates from an instinctual bond existing between mother and child. The relationships cultivated between parents and children, as well as the manner in which they are cultivated, are seen to be private matters based on the culture and personality of the family itself, including its ethnic, racial, religious, and political values. In a pluralist society where diversity in this value orientation exists—and to some degree is celebrated—it is difficult to imagine a unitary family-related policy or program that would equally represent all interests. Furthermore, the family is the one social institution in which this diversity can be expressed without the judgment or interference of others—so long as it remains a privatized institution.

Public programs of a family nature, such as child care, assault this ideology and threaten our sense of privacy. Therefore, they are resisted on many grounds. As the following chapter shows, ideological assumptions about mothering and family privacy historically have dominated public responses to child care needs in the United States. Government programs have been established only in cases where women are perceived to have "failed" in their natural duties, or where a national economic or political emergency has called for public involvement. As we will see, this is one reason why, in the face of a clear and growing need, we are now turning not to government to provide child care services but to employers.

NOTES

1. The number of families headed by never-married mothers grew 356 percent in the 1970s (U.S. Commission on Civil Rights 1983).

2. By "quality" I mean attention to the individual personality and needs of a child, fostering social as well as intellectual development among children, and providing a safe and caring environment for children.

3. For a critique of the "mothering mandate," see Russo 1979.

4. For reviews of evaluative research on child care, see Dally 1982; Rutter 1982; Scarr 1984; Silverstein 1981.

5. For discussions of comparative family policy, including child care, see Adams and Winston 1980; Kamerman and Kahn 1978, 1981.

6. See Piven and Cloward 1982.

Chapter 2

A History of Child Care Policies and Programs

Even with the kinds of ideological resistance described in the last chapter, the United States has had some kind of extrafamilial child care sponsored by government or employers—or the two in cooperation—since the early nineteenth century. This chapter looks at the conditions under which child care programs have been developed. An overview of the history of child care policies and programs reveals that since the early nineteenth century, the focus of government-sponsored child care programs has been on income maintenance for the poor and, sometimes in collaboration with industry, control over female employment in peace-time and wartime economies.

On the whole, child care has been provided by government to certain families only when it is linked to larger social problems of unemployment, disadvantage, or disaster. Thus, both the programs and the people using them have been stigmatized: Extrafamilial child care has been either something "remedial" for "deficient" families, or an "expedient" in "emergency" situations. Until very recently, child care has not been considered appropriate or necessary for the majority of "normal," intact, middle class families. While there now appears to be a shift toward greater public acceptance of child care for anyone who desires it, the stigma of government programs remains. This, I believe, is one major reason we are turning to employers to provide child care instead of to government.

We can identify three traditions in child care arrangements involving government and/or private organizations in the United

States since the nineteenth century: day care, nursery school, and compensatory education (Gerald 1972). Each of these traditions has had a different programmatic emphasis and serves a different population of parents and children.

Day care historically has existed to provide supervision of children of working parents, particularly low income and welfare mothers, and its emphasis is therefore custodial. The nursery school was established to provide an enriching educational experience to children of more affluent parents supplementary to family life, and has emphasized child development rather than supervision. Finally, compensatory education programs, such as Head Start, represent an attempt to provide compensatory experiences to impoverished and minority children who are perceived to be at an educational disadvantage compared with their more affluent counterparts. The idea is to "even up" the competition for future educational and occupational opportunities.

Taking these traditions together, Gerald (1972: 269) summarizes: "Our long term tradition of day care in America is one of supervision for the children of working mothers and 'enrichment' for the children of non-working parents who can afford it."

The following historical review discusses the circumstances under which these different types of programs have emerged and how they have affected one another to form our current image and supply of child care.

NINETEENTH-EARLY TWENTIETH CENTURY: INFANT SCHOOLS AND DAY NURSERIES

The first expression of day care programs in the United States was the infant schools established around 1830 (Greenblatt 1977). These were organized by philanthropists and catered to the children of poor and immigrant families. The very name of these institutions implies that they had educational, not just custodial, goals.

Although there is no direct evidence, it is probable that the development of the infant schools was linked to the emerging concern for child welfare and represented real desires to mitigate some of the social and economic hardships to which many children were exposed. Whatever their pedagogic character, infant schools had significance as "the first *secular* expression of social parenthood" (Greenblatt 1977: 20).

At nearly the same time, government involvement in child care began in a small way with the day nurseries that emerged as a response to the wave of immigration occurring between 1815 and 1840, to industrialization, and to the factory employment of women. Like the infant schools, day nurseries were tied to social welfare concerns about both child neglect and societal disorganization (Greenblatt 1977; Kerr 1973; Steinfels 1973).

Modeled after the French crèche, day nurseries were, on the whole, privately owned, philanthropic ventures staffed by affluent women. The first reportedly was opened in 1838 by Mrs. Joseph Hale for the children of wives and widows of seamen (Kerr 1973). Subsequently, day nurseries were opened in medical facilities in New York City in 1854; in Troy, New York, in 1858; for female workers in Philadelphia during the Civil War (1863); and at the Chicago World's Fair in 1898. In fact, by 1898, there were 175 day nurseries in operation in the United States, a phenomenon that warranted the creation of the National Federation of Day Nurseries. While most of the nurseries were privately financed, some did receive state support. For example, the state of Maryland donated $3,000 in 1901 to two nurseries in Baltimore (Kerr 1973).

The proliferation of day nurseries was tied to the increasing pressure on poor mothers to work outside the home as capitalist industry intensified. Thus, the day nurseries had the double aim of preventing child neglect and alleviating some of the hardships faced by working mothers. In addition, they had a larger goal: to preserve and strengthen the family (Greenblatt 1977; Steinfels 1973). Steinfels (1973:44) suggests that because of their population of poor children, the day nurseries "considered themselves a substitute for home and mother; in some cases, a substitute better than home and mother." A large proportion of the day nurseries' clientele were immigrant children who were directed there to relieve the rolls at more costly public social welfare institutions. This gave the programs a socializing function as well. For example, California's public school nurseries, which opened after a compulsory education law was passed in 1910, explicitly had as part of their design the "Americanization" of immigrant children (Kerr 1973:159).

Whether the day nurseries were for children of working mothers or of immigrants, their users were stigmatized for being in a position of need. This attitude prevented the day nurseries from ever really achieving acceptance as an institution. Social workers criticized the programs for having bad health standards and for having family-weakening, rather than strengthening, implications (Kerr 1973; Steinfels 1973).

The latter argument was based on the assumption that extra-familial maternal employment, no matter how necessary, was inappropriate for women and detrimental to families and children. Therefore, in the beginning, day nurseries apparently accepted only children whose fathers were absent or permanently incapacitated, for these children's dire circumstances could easily justify maternal employment in the minds of the public. "In such tragic cases, departure from the normative family pattern could be condoned" (Greenblatt 1977:22).

Thus, the general attitude of social workers toward the day nurseries by the early twentieth century was framed in relation to the ideal of the nonpathological family: "The day nursery was consequently only a temporary expedient until family life could be reconstructed and the mother restored to her rightful place at home" (Steinfels 1973:62). This began a long process of change in the day nursery from a broadly defined child care service to "a marginal and limited agent of social welfare" (Steinfels 1973:63).

The revelation by social workers that child care institutions—public and private—often provided minimal care and allowed for abuse of children stirred public sentiment and provoked a reaction by the federal government. President Theodore Roosevelt convened the first White House Conference on Children in 1909 to discuss the care of dependent children. In its first resolution, the Conference declared:

Home life is the highest and finest product of civilization. . . . [Unfortunate children of worthy parents] should as a rule be kept with their parents, [with] aid being given as may be necessary to maintain suitable homes for the rearing of the children. . . . Except in unusual circumstances, the home should not be broken up for reasons of poverty, but only for reasons of inefficiency or immorality. (quoted in Bremner 1971:365)

The Conference proposed not federal, but state, aid programs by which children could be taken care of in their own homes through "private charity rather than public relief." Although there was strong opposition from social service traditionalists, the Conference recommended, and eventually saw 40 states adopt, what became known as mothers' pension laws after 1911. The pension was essentially a support payment to enable women to stay home and care for their own children.

Eligibility for the mothers' pension was limited by family structure and the potential wage earning ability of the mother. Generally speaking, pensions were limited to wives and children of deceased, incapacitated, insane, or imprisoned men. And, while unskilled or semiskilled mothers were eligible, those who were skilled or could potentially earn a good wage were not: "A class distinction, in other words, was built into the mothers' pension programs" (Greenblatt 1977:38).

The existence of mothers' aid legislation affected the nature of day nurseries. The nurseries experienced declining enrollments among their original population—children of widows—and began accepting children of two working parents. Additionally, for those mothers who chose to work, the day nurseries provided an alternative to the pensions and were thus perceived as a substitute for, or even a form of, public relief. Day care began to define itself in these terms. As Greenblatt (1977) argues:

By becoming attached to the relief system day care came to share the stigma of that system. This produced lasting effects on day-care programs and public policy in subsequent epochs. For these reasons, the decade of mothers' pension programs decisively influenced the development of day care. Furthermore, the aid legislation also established the subsidizing of mothers to stay home and rear their children as the predominant public policy in the various states. (p. 39)

WORLD WAR I

Accounts of child care during World War I are sparse. There is some evidence that the Women's Committee of the Council of National Defense discussed the possibility of establishing day nurseries in manufacturing areas. But apparently no action was taken, and day care needs created by wartime employment of women were met in centers operated on an ad hoc basis (Kerr 1973). It is possible that the federal government did not aid in establishing day care centers for mothers in war production partly because the country's involvement in the war lasted only 18 months (Greenblatt 1977).

This is not to say there was no need or demand for child care. On the contrary, women were one-quarter of the work force when the United States entered the war, and their number increased by 1 million between 1915 and 1919. Therefore, it seems reasonable to assume that there was an increased need for day care in general during the war. In fact, some industrial day care centers were established, but most closed right after the war. Although costliness may be the common reason given for their closure, an alternative explanation is suggested in the words of a public speaker of the day who stated: "Women have responded with fine patriotism to the appeal to take part in industry during the war. It now becomes their duty to withdraw" (quoted in Greenblatt 1977:40). After the war, both day care and women's labor force participation were seen to be neither necessary nor appropriate.

During this same period, the nursery school movement emerged. Kerr (1973) argues that this was in response to the popular belief that problems in early childhood had caused the physical or mental deficiencies that disqualified many men for military service during World War I. The first nursery school was opened in 1915 by a group of faculty wives at the University of Chicago. In the 1920s, a number of experimental nursery school programs were set up for research in child care and development in such locations as New York, Detroit, Boston, and the universities of Iowa, Minnesota, and California.

The American nursery school movement was influenced by European models developed by Friedrich Froebel, Maria Montessori, and even the utopian socialist Robert Owen. But the clientele differed. While, for example, Owen's school in Scotland served working class and poor children, American models of it and of other nursery school programs served children of primarily middle class and well educated families.

Although professionals in the nursery school movement attempted to distinguish their programs from the day nurseries, this was not entirely possible. In fact, nursery schools had both a positive and a negative effect on day nurseries. On the one hand, Kerr (1973) notes:

Because the nursery school movement stressed the advantage of some group experience for children outside the home and proved the point by providing environments superior to many homes, it may have made a gentle dent in the fears that surrounded the practice of separating the child from its mother for any part of the day. (p. 161)

As a result, all day care may have been viewed more positively. But, on the other hand, the nursery school movement generally viewed day nurseries with contempt, as it thought of them as a service to socially pathological families. This negative image was already held by many people, and was intensified once the nursery school had become popular with the middle class and with established educational institutions. Consequently, public support and private funding for day nurseries waned.

THE GREAT DEPRESSION: WPA

The next significant development in public child care occurred during the Great Depression. In 1933, as part of President Roosevelt's Federal Emergency Relief Act and later the Works Progress Administration (WPA), federally financed day nurseries and nursery schools were established. Roosevelt's intent was to pull people off relief by creating jobs for unemployed teachers, nurses, cooks, janitors, and nutritionists (Greenblatt 1977; Kerr 1973). Indeed, "The preschool programs were not designed principally to provide child care for working mothers, but to provide employment for preschool teachers and other personnel. The preschool programs for children served only as a secondary purpose" (Greenblatt 1977:55).

Because of the Depression context, the WPA day care programs served to blur much of the distinction between the clientele of day nurseries and nursery schools. Although they were explicitly designed for children from families on relief, during the Depression a majority of people were relatively impoverished. Additionally, as Greenblatt (1977:55) points out, "despite the employment *purpose* of the programs, their *content* was clearly defined as education." So the relief assumptions of the day nurseries and the educational emphasis of nursery schools were combined in the WPA programs. Underscoring the educational component is the fact that two-thirds of the programs were located in public schools. In 1937, 40,000 children were enrolled in an estimated 1,500–1,900 WPA child care programs (Clarke-Stewart 1982; Greenblatt 1977). This represented an unprecedented increase in the number of children served by government child care, and according to Kerr (1973:162), "It represented the first federal recognition that the education and guidance of young children was a responsibility warranting the appropriation of public funds."

In a separate but perhaps related development, in 1935, Title V of the Social Security Act was passed, which allowed for grants-in-aid for child care services and research. Funds for these programs were administered through departments of public welfare, a "precedent of much greater consequence for the future identity of day care than the WPA" (Kerr 1973:162).

In fact, with the demise of the WPA in 1938, public day nurseries and nursery schools declined until World War II, indicating that local schools lacked a sense of vested interest or responsibility for preschool education.

WORLD WAR II: GOVERNMENT AND INDUSTRY COLLABORATION

A few years later, an even more significant turn of events than the Depression affected the nation's attitude toward publicly sponsored child care—World War II. It was during the war that the first example of government-industry collaboration in child care appeared. Since this experience clearly illustrates the tensions between the labor force needs of government and industry and American cultural ideals about working women—and how these tensions are played out in child care policy—it is important to discuss it in some detail here.

When women first started working during World War II, day care facilities were limited, and the alternative arrangements many mothers made for their children were often unreliable and unsafe. Ideological resistance to enlarging the role of government in child care still remained.

But by the final years of the war, the tremendous growth in female employment warranted some type of government response. Between 1940 and 1944, female employment increased by an estimated 51 percent. Twenty percent of women with children under 18 years old and 12.5 percent of women with children under age 6 were working. In March 1944, more than half of the married women whose husbands were away at war worked, as did one-fifth of those whose husbands were at home (National Manpower Council 1957). Women workers' need for child care, generally ignored by the government before these high levels of female employment, now became a salient concern because it was directly linked to the stabilization of the female labor force and to maintenance of wartime production levels.

Yet government child care policy that did emerge was generally incoherent, fragmented, and based upon the assumption that public-supported child care—and female employment generally—was only a temporary necessity, strictly a wartime measure. This is in part a result of the presumption that the majority of workers in war-related industries would be middle class women who entered the labor force temporarily as part of the war effort, and who would leave the labor force voluntarily— to return to "normal family life"—after the war had ended.

Actually, the majority of women war industry laborers were from the working class. These were women who had been working before the war and who left clerical, service, domestic, and other types of low skilled, low paid "women's" jobs for higher status, higher paying jobs in war goods manufacture (Dratch

1974; Frank et al. 1982; Honey 1984). Two-thirds of the women at work during the war had been working beforehand, and most intended to continue working after the war. A 1944 survey by the United Auto Workers indicated that 85 percent of the women in the union wished to keep their jobs after the war (Frank et al. 1982; Tobias and Anderson 1973). This figure included 100 percent of the UAW women who were widows, 99 percent of the single women, and 69 percent of the married women (Frank et al. 1982).

A broader survey of 13,000 women conducted by the Women's Bureau in 1944–1945 found that 75 percent intended to keep their jobs after the war ended. Among those who had not been employed or looking for employment previous to the war, 75 percent of young women (just out of school) and 50 percent of older women (chiefly housewives) expected to keep working. Furthermore, the survey showed, 87 percent of the single, 94 percent of the divorced or widowed, and 57 percent of the married women intended to remain employed after the war (National Manpower Council 1957). In fact, it has been estimated that as many as 80 percent of women working during the war continued to do so immediately afterward, although most were pushed back into lower paid, traditionally female work (Frank et al. 1982; Gregory 1974). Nevertheless, the government assumed otherwise when developing child care policy and programs during and after the war.

Within federal government agencies, there was much debate about the appropriateness of federally sponsored child care. Strong opposition existed within the Federal Security Agency, the U.S. Children's Bureau, the U.S. Office of Education, and, initially, the War Manpower Commission (Dratch 1974). Much of their opposition was on ideological grounds and reflected the prevailing notion that child care was an individual, at-home responsibility not to be transferred to the state. Specifically, as Dratch (1974:170) points out, "Underlying the debate was the question of to what extent the war-time emergency was to be allowed to disrupt traditional patterns of family life, child rearing, and women in the home."

But, as the war continued, the need to mobilize women for

defense production increased to such a degree that even with this opposition, the federal government acknowledged a responsibility to provide child care. Yet, the ideological and economic rationalizations for keeping women in the home still acted as a brake on its involvement.

Federal involvement in child care was accomplished most directly by the passage of the Lanham Act (Public Law 137) in 1941. This was a public works bill that included child care (although it did somewhat as an afterthought). Beginning in 1942, under the administration of the Federal Works Agency (FWA), Lanham funds were allocated on a community basis to set up child care centers in defense plants employing women. Communities were expected to provide 50 percent of the operating costs through parent fees or local contributions, and they were obliged to prove the existence of their child care need. As Lanham funds were applicable only to "war-impact areas," these communities had to prove that their child care problem "was caused or increased by war programs, that large numbers of women were being employed, and that local financing could not meet the community's needs" (Anderson 1981:124). But many communities were ill equipped to take on the financial and bureaucratic burdens entailed in establishing programs, and only if they were in dire financial need would the FWA pay more than its usual 50 percent.

Ultimately, $51,922,977 in federal and $26,008,839 in state funds were disbursed under the Lanham Act for the development nationwide of 3,102 community centers serving a total of about 600,000 children (Kerr 1973).[1] Although this sounds impressive, it is estimated that these centers served only 40 percent of the children in need of care (Kerr 1973; Steiner 1976). In Los Angeles alone, for example, the 21 centers operating in 1943 served 2,000 children while an estimated 8,000 needed care. Truly fulfilling this need would have required 197 centers (Gregory 1974).

From the beginning, the FWA program was resisted by government agencies, unions, employers, and social welfare agents, for different but sometimes overlapping reasons. This is how Dratch (1974) describes the situation:

The F.S.A. (Federal Security Agency), and its allied agencies, along with the National Welfare League of America, lobbied to discourage group child care for working class mothers and to encourage them to find individual care. They were joined by numerous employers who shared their fears that women could permanently overload the labor market and that child care would create too high a tax burden. Child Welfare officials were especially wary of the rapid and innovative growth of the F.W.A.'s group child care centers, saying they feared such facilities would harm the mother-child relationship by creating an undesirable decline in parent contact. (p. 179)

Consequently, from its inception, the FWA program was limited by the notion within Congress that federal money for child care was allotted solely as a war emergency effort. A statement in the 1946 Annual Report of the FWA makes this clear:

Child care never before had been considered to be a public responsibility, and the committee's approval was predicated exclusively on a war-connected emergency need. That need would cease to exist when Japan surrendered, and promptly upon the consummation of that event the Federal Works Agency was to retire completely and irrevocably from the child-care field. (quoted in Dratch 1974:176–177)

This is precisely what happened. Although 47 states participated in the FWA program, only one—California—picked up the funding and maintained its centers after the program was dismantled in 1948. Summarizing the government's Lanham Act involvement, Steiner (1976:16) says: "It does not suggest any major deviation from the general nonintervention tradition . . . it was a win-the-war program, not a save-the-children program."

Industry Sponsored Child Care

It was during this same period—World War II—that private industry became directly involved in providing child care; and it did so for much the same reason that government did—to employ women more efficiently during the crisis. And, like government, industry perceived its role in child care to be a temporary, emergency measure only. In fact, the two collaborated on the question of female employment and the provision of child care both during the war and immediately after it.

As a general rule, war industries avoided taking responsibility for the care of children of female employees, perceiving it to be a responsibility of the workers themselves or of the community. Kaiser Industries Corporation was one well-publicized exception to this rule. Of 12,000 female employees in its Oregon shipyards, one-third were mothers with no child care options, prompting the company to develop on-site centers (Canon 1978). Highly touted as "model," the Kaiser child care program consisted of two centers, at the Swan Island and the Oregonship shipyards in Portland. The centers operated from 1943 to 1945 and served a total of 4,019 children. At their peak operating point in the summer of 1944, they were open 24 hours a day and served 444 children at Swan Island and 390 children at Oregonship per day. Services at the centers were extensive and included education, psychology, social work, nutrition, infirmaries, and even hot take-home food (Dratch 1974; Canon 1978).

While the child care efforts of Kaiser were seen by many as commendable, they were also profitable to the company. The cost of the Kaiser program was considerable, but it was passed on almost entirely to the public sector. The buildings were paid for by the U.S. Maritime Commission, the centers received Lanham Act funds, and other expenses were covered under the cost-plus contract system, through which expenses for employee services were added into the cost of producing the ships and then passed on to the Department of War. The closest thing to corporate money that went into the program was the fees paid by employee parents from their salaries. These fees were slightly higher than those charged in other Lanham Act centers but lower than those of other local day nurseries (Dratch 1974).

The Kaiser program probably was possible in large part because it did not cost the corporation anything. On the contrary, enabling the stable employment of such vast numbers of women increased Kaiser's profits. And having federal funds pay for corporate expansion and employee services made wartime (and later, peacetime) business quite lucrative. As Dratch (1974:198) puts it, "War may have been a disaster for many, but it was a bonanza for the corporate shipbuilding yards." A congressional investigation report, "Economic Concentration in World War II," shows that about half of the federal war production expenditures ($616 million) was allocated for expanding private shipbuilding and manufacturing facilities. This provided the companies, at no cost, the infrastructure that enabled them to reap big profits in the postwar economy (Dratch 1974). The child care program during the war was just part of this bonanza for Kaiser; and, as described above, it was funded in a way that distinguished it as strictly a wartime measure. In fact, the resident director of the Kaiser child care program, James L. Hymes, Jr., was a member of the War Department.

At this same time, a few other scattered war industries established child care programs. Among these were a tank plant in Peoria, Illinois, a tent and uniform manufacturing shop in Cleveland, Ohio, and the Curtiss-Wright Corporation in Buffalo (Frank et. al. 1982). Other industries pushed for expanded community child care, for instance, the Douglas Aircraft Corporation in Los Angeles—the largest private employer of women in the nation during the war. The Los Angeles aircraft plants found that they suffered serious womanpower losses at the time of school vacations. The West Coast Aircraft War Production Council calculated what these losses meant to the total war effort: "One child care center enabling 40 mothers to work full shifts adds up to 8000 manhours a month. . . . Lack of 25 child care centers can cost ten bombers a month" (*Business Week*, Aug. 21, 1943:88–89).

The language of this statement reflects the primary concern behind industry support of public and private child care: to keep production levels high during the war by stabilizing the female labor force. As Miriam Lowenberg (1944:77), chief nutritionist of the Kaiser child service department, wrote: "We are constantly reminding ourselves that the primary purpose of these schools is the stabilization of the woman shipyard worker"— and not, one presumes, the care of children. Like the government-sponsored FWA child care programs, industry programs were created with production goals in mind and were perceived as a wartime emergency measure, only "for the duration." Consequently, when the war ended in 1945, Kaiser's centers were rapidly closed. This occurred even though parents protested and even though the *Final Report* of the Kaiser Child Service Centers stated so positively: "It seems clear that the centers have proved that child care facilities can contribute to production . . . and can be operated by industry to the great advantage of children and parents and to the benefit of industry" (quoted in Canon 1978:86).

The nationwide closure of public (FWA) child care centers after the war also was not accomplished without resistance. Working women in many cities petitioned, demonstrated, and lobbied their unions and elected officials to try to keep the child care centers open (Dratch 1974; Frank et al. 1982). Yet in most cases their efforts proved futile, as it was never the government's intention to view its support of child care during the war as anything other than expedient. The primary goal of federally funded child care in wartime was to increase productivity rather than to serve working women and their children.

Not only did most child care centers close at the end of the war, but a great number of women left the labor force. Approximately one out of six (or 2 million) women in the labor force in 1941 had left by 1944 (National Manpower Council 1957).[2] In 1945, 3.25 million women out of 18 million in the work force left their jobs, and 500,000 of them never found work again (Frank et al. 1982). While we have seen that it was the explicit intention of government and industry to treat the wartime employment of women as extraordinary and temporary, it is so far unclear how and why women accepted this idea and left the labor force, especially given the occupational mobility many working class women experienced for the first time.

Government and Media Collaboration

In *Creating Rosie the Riveter*, Maureen Honey (1984) convincingly shows how the propaganda wing of the government, the Office of War Information (OWI), was effective in disseminating through popular culture its attitude about the temporary nature of female employment.[3] The OWI published and distributed the *War Magazine Guide*, which informed magazine publishers of current government policies and provided suggestions on how they could support these policies in magazine content. Both the middle-class-oriented *Saturday Evening Post* and the working-class-oriented *True Story* strongly reinforced the image of the woman war worker as a temporary laborer inspired by patriotic motivation. Rather than replacing the dominant image of women as homemakers with one of women as productive employees, media combined these two functions in what Honey terms a reactionary ideology of female service to the family, modesty, self-abnegation, feminine virtue, and maternal altruism. Often the interests of the nation were identified with the survival of the traditional American family. Additionally, the image of women working not for themselves but for their nation and for "the boys on the front" reinforced both the temporary nature of their work and the role of women as selfless, unambitious beings devoted to the welfare of others.

Magazines were also deliberate, yet not unanimous, in their portrayal of public supported child care centers. Some—the more middle class—portrayed child care centers favorably. Others—mostly working class magazines—gave child care programs very little support; in fact, *True Story* refrained from any reference to them at all (Honey 1984).[4]

In short, popular women's magazines reflected government assumptions about the temporary nature of the wartime female labor force and its emphasis on preserving family values. They also reflected the government's ambiguity regarding public-supported child care. In both, these magazines served to inculcate that attitude among employed women themselves and thereby assisted in provoking their departure from the labor force immediately after the war.

The Role of Unions

Images in popular culture were not the only forces militating against the permanent presence of women in the labor force and of child care institutions established to support them. Even the unions that represented female workers in an unprecedented fashion during the war were not advocates for them after it. On the contrary, they, too, argued that it was women's "duty" to give their jobs back to men returning from the war.

In fact, unions played a very interesting role in the question of working women and child care during this period. Like government and the popular media, their activities reflected ambivalence about both phenomena.

Between 1939 and 1945, women's membership in unions grew from 800,000 to over 3 million—about 22 percent of total union membership (National Manpower Council 1957). The surge was in great part due to the movement of women workers from traditionally "female," nonunion jobs in the clerical, sales, domestic, teaching, and nursing fields to traditionally "male," union manufacturing jobs during the war. Many of the industrial plants that women workers entered were covered by collective bargaining agreements and "maintenance of membership" policies, whereby these new workers automatically became members (Frank et al. 1982). Other women became union members when their plants were organized in 1944 (National Manpower Council 1957).

As a response to the influx of women, some of the larger unions, such as the United Automobile Workers (UAW), established Women's Bureaus or committees to address their particular concerns. The UAW and United Electrical, Radio and Machine Workers of America developed policies to protect women workers on issues of equal pay, seniority, work standards, and maternity leave. Recognizing women's double burden of employment and household responsibilities, the CIO publicized the need for day care, lobbied in Congress for adequate funding, and worked with community groups to establish local centers (S. Hartmann 1982).

But there were two limitations to unions' advocacy in this period that had serious consequences for women workers once the war ended (and, one could argue, still do today). First, there were very few women in leadership positions within unions, which made women dependent upon men to protect their interests (interests that, as we will see, potentially conflicted with men's). For example, in 1944, when women were 30 percent of total membership, the UAW listed fewer than 50 women out of more than 2,000 convention delegates. Even at the local level, although better than the national, women's representation in leadership positions was minimal. There, Susan Hartmann

(1982:65) notes, "Of those UAW locals having women members, 60 percent had at least one woman on their executive boards, but women did less well on the important bargaining and grievance committees. Only on 37 percent of the former and 24 percent of the latter were women represented at all."

The second limitation on unions' effectiveness in assisting women workers during the war was the resistance by male workers to women's presence, and their sustained belief that women's employment was, and should be, temporary. Even where equal pay gains were made, they were supported "largely in order to preserve a high wage scale for returning veterans" (Frank et al. 1982:36). A UAW official, speaking to women at a convention in 1943, made this point clear when he said: "It is your job to maintain the unions and to see that the men have good conditions to come back to" (quoted in Frank et al. 1982:36).

The protection of wages was a grave concern to union men who had fought hard for it before the war. Over the years, unions had battled many employers who attempted, and often succeeded, in bringing in female workers at lower wages. The fear among men workers during the war was that this would happen again. Thus, when women began entering male occupations, "The initial attitude of many male workers, unorganized as well as organized, was suspicion, if not outright hostility" (National Manpower Council 1957:152). In fact, not only were men worried about decreased wage standards, they were also worried about job security. Many feared there would be widespread unemployment after the war, and that their own future job security was jeopardized by the massive employment of women (S. Hartmann 1982).

But in the end, these men had very little to worry about. Even with equal pay policies,[5] unions could, and did, use seniority systems to protect the long term interests of men and to discriminate between male and female workers. Ultimately, "When rank and file men union members recognized that they were given preference for upgrading and promotion and that their security was being protected, they felt much less defensive about the large-scale invasion by women" (National Manpower Council 1957:152–153). At the same time, unions assumed that women's employment was temporary, and their contracts often contained clauses that limited women's stay or seniority and gave job retention priority to men when layoffs were imminent. After the war, women workers were laid off at a rate 75 percent higher than men (Frank et al. 1982). Karen Anderson (1981) neatly summarizes the behavior of unions during the latter years of the war:

They acquiesced in the violation of supposedly sacrosanct principles, especially those involving seniority-based job security and promotion, when such practices meant a preference for male workers in skilled job categories and enhanced the possibility that women would be excluded from "male" jobs once the war was over. The long-term needs of male workers took precedence over the prerogatives of women workers, as the postwar period would soon demonstrate. (p. 60)

And demonstrate it did. The attitudes of employers, unions, and male workers paralleled those of the government and its propaganda wing, the OWI, by stressing the temporary nature of female employment. Rather than being cast as an expression of liberation and independence, the wartime employment of women was seen as an emergency measure for the security and defense of the nation. Rather than fully incorporating women into the labor force and providing incentives for them to stay, the activities of government, industry, and unions underscored the belief that the true and proper place for a woman was in the home, and that it was her duty to relinquish her wartime job to its "rightful" male owner upon the country's return to normalcy. Consequently, none of these interests lobbied after the war for the protection of policies and programs initiated during it to accommodate women workers. Child care was one such casualty. Government funding for FWA centers was terminated in 1948; Kaiser and other industries closed their centers in 1945; and unions failed to fight either of these developments with any conviction.

1950s: ANTI-COMMUNAL SENTIMENTS

The 1950s are generally viewed as the decade in which the nuclear family as we know it became firmly entrenched, with the effective removal of many women from the labor force and a massive propaganda campaign glorifying the virtues of house-wifery. Although in 1950 4.6 million mothers worked, there was very little activity—public or private—in support of child care services for them. There are different interpretations of this inactivity.

Dratch (1974) suggests that the dominant explanation from social welfare sources about the demise of wartime child care programs was that a lack of communication existed among so-cial workers, educators, politicians, and working mothers about the sustained need. He argues that this apparent "information gap" was in fact a deliberate attempt by social welfare agencies to protect their power over local child care programs from con-trol by the federal government. Dratch's own position is that the failure to continue or extend child care services after the war was more directly related to the needs of capitalist industry to keep women as a reserve—and not a regular—labor pool: "If provided with better child care services, for example, black and working class mothers might be less inclined to work for low pay under demeaning conditions" (1974, p. 203). He fur-ther argues that spending on social services was not as profita-ble to capitalism as was military spending. Thus, he locates the lack of support for social services, especially those for working mothers, in "the capitalist structure of the economy itself."

Kerr (1973) offers a different explanation for the lack of support for child care after the war—the anti-Communist fury dominant at the time:

Whatever effort there might have been during the period to promote increased public support of day care was stilled by the strong senti-ment against the working mother and by community suspicion of pro-grams that seemed to extend the powers of the state. Fear of com-munism touched all areas of life, and—the U.S. war and depression programs notwithstanding—the child care center was regarded in some parts as a Russian invention. (p. 166).

Probably for both economic and ideological reasons, little government activity on child care occurred during the 1950s. Even though women reentered defense industries during the

Korean War, no support was given by the federal government to aid in the establishment of community day care facilities. Federal administrators in fact saw child care as a local concern and responsibility, and they were unwilling to involve federal funds in anything more than supplementary amounts. In the absence of organized lobbying, and with the fulfillment in 1952 of President Eisenhower's campaign promise to end the Korean War, defense-related child care became moot (Steiner 1976).

In the following years, nothing much occurred until 1958, when Jacob Javits, Republican senator from New York, proposed a bill to provide day care for working mothers. But in the end, not much came of this or any other of the Cold War child care bills that were introduced during this period.

EARLY 1960s: RELIEVING THE WELFARE ROLES

The 1960s saw a surge in concern about child care, but little real activity. As in former years, policy recommendations reflected the view of child care as an "unpleasant necessity" for certain kinds of families. In 1960, the Women's Bureau and Children's Bureau cosponsored a National Conference on Day Care for Children at which recommendations were made for local, state, and federal funding for child care. These recommendations were given a boost by President-elect Kennedy, who spoke out in favor of day care centers for "children of working mothers and of parents who for one reason and another cannot provide adequate care during the day" (quoted in Steiner 1976:21).

One year later, in 1961, Kennedy sent a welfare message to Congress, attempting to establish services to get people off welfare assistance. Included in this message was a request for authorization of $5 million the first year and $10 million thereafter for aiding local child care programs and for developing new ones. In 1963, appropriations were finally granted, although only in the amount of $800,000. This represented the first federal financial assistance for child care purposes since 1946.

Like the earlier WPA programs, the attempt was to get women

off welfare rather than to provide a service to children. The program was tied primarily to low income working or disabled women. Indeed, throughout the time between the Lanham Act and Kennedy's child care program, "in each case, enabling part of the population to work, not improving child development, was the public policy objective" (Steiner 1976:22).

MID-1960s: HEAD START

During the mid-1960s the interests of children began to enter the child care debate. Child development became an issue with new research on the question of whether intelligence is genetically fixed or is affected by environmental stimulation. Benjamin Bloom's (1964) work on the pattern of intelligence development was most influential.

Bloom's research showed that rapid development occurs in a child's early years—up to age five—and then begins to slow: By age four, one has accounted for approximately 50 percent of the variation in general intelligence possible for any one child. This research emphasized the importance a child's environment plays in the development of his or her intelligence. Assuming that environments can be manipulated, Bloom's findings had great implications for child care policy. From that point on, "Child care centers were more than a matter of maternal convenience or a technique for reducing welfare costs. Potentially, at least, they were investments in human development and could become instruments of social change" (Steiner 1976:25).

This attitude served as the impetus, in 1964, for Project Head Start, the large-scale government effort to engage in compensatory educational programs for environmentally and economically disadvantaged children. However, once again, it was not solely concern for children's development that motivated policy makers to initiate the Head Start Program. Rather, the program was seen as part of a larger political goal shared by Presidents Kennedy and Johnson: to combat poverty in America.

Project Head Start was part of the Economic Opportunity Act (Public Law 88-452) and the War on Poverty program of the Johnson administration. The idea of the project was to give poor and ghetto-dwelling preschool age children a supplementary education that would better prepare them to compete in public schools with their more environmentally advantaged peers. Ultimately, the aim of Head Start was to "interrupt the cycle of poverty at the lower age level" (Greenblatt 1977:211).

But this broad, long-term goal produced a number of short-term problems that, from its inception, formed the basis for criticism of Head Start. First, the model focused solely on organized centers serving preschool age children; that is, no alternatives such as in-home service, child development training for parents, or prenatal care were considered. Second, it was discovered that many of the effects of Head Start were negated once children entered public schools, although it is not altogether clear why. And finally, although children were exposed to enriching educational experiences in the centers, they returned to their disadvantaged homes and environments, which some scholars thought had adverse effects on what was being attempted in Head Start (Greenblatt 1977; Steiner 1976).

Even with these criticisms, Head Start did have a positive effect on the public's attitude toward extrafamilial child care, and showed that public programs for children as young as three could be established. In short, it gave out-of-home child care a measure of intellectual respectability.

Nevertheless, because Head Start, like its predecessors, was essentially an antipoverty program, and because poverty is linked with welfare dependency, the stigma of public child care as being appropriate only for "relief from relief" remained. Even though its stated aim was educational parity for children, ultimately it was an antipoverty program for adults that didn't—and couldn't—really work as such. At least, it couldn't work in one generation and by itself. Lacking the level of measurable success expected of it, Project Head Start—although still existing in some parts of the country—did not engender further educational child care programs for a broader population, as many had hoped it would.

1970s: THE VETO OF COMPREHENSIVE CHILD CARE

In the late 1960s and early 1970s a number of proposals for public child care programs were made at different levels of government, but few were adopted. The most significant of these proposals was the 1971 Comprehensive Child Development Act, an attempt to legitimize public involvement and federal money in child care. The bill was "comprehensive" in the sense that it combined Walter Mondale's proposal in the Senate to expand Head Start and assist more children from low income and poverty areas, and John Brademas's proposal in the House to provide preschool educational programs to children who needed them in order to "realize their full potential" (not just those in low income families). The bill provided for a sliding scale of fees to be paid by parents, including middle income parents, according to their ability to pay. There would be free child care for families with incomes below the poverty level established by the Bureau of Labor Statistics.

Supporters were optimistic about the chances of the bill passing because of statements made earlier by President Nixon. In his "Message on Reorganization of the War on Poverty" in 1969, Nixon had emphasized a "national commitment to providing all American children an opportunity for healthful and stimulating development during the first five years of life." But two years later, after the Mondale-Brademas bill had passed both the Senate and the House, President Nixon vetoed it. Although there was no indication at the time that a veto was forthcoming, there are different explanations for it.

Nixon's veto speech indicated that his opposition to the bill was ideological—government-supported comprehensive child care would undermine the American family: "For the Federal Government to plunge headlong financially into supporting child development would commit the vast moral authority of the National Government to the side of communal approaches to child rearing over against the family-centered approach" (quoted in Adams and Winston 1980:67). Nixon seemed to be responding to his own deep-seated distaste for communal child care.

But it is also possible that while the specific language of the veto message represented the president's own ideological resistance to child care, the anti-communal theme actually had larger significance: to appease right wing critics of Nixon's recent China policy. In other words, the child development bill may have been sacrificed to reconfirm Nixon's anti-Communist image, which had been questioned by hard-liners when he reopened relations with China in the same year (1971). The link between extrafamilial child care and Communism was obviously something perceived by many people besides President Nixon.

Mondale and Brademas attempted to reintroduce their bill in a scaled-down version in 1974, as the Child and Family Services Act, and again in 1975. In both cases, the sliding fee scale for child care—with free services for poor families—was retained. But in neither case were the sponsors successful in getting their bill passed.

In all, about 15 to 20 child care bills have been presented to Congress every session since 1971. Only a few have passed, and none of them provides comprehensive child care. Furthermore, the federally funded programs that remained into this period have been drastically cut under the Reagan administration (as described in Chapter 1).

So far, I have argued that from the early day nurseries, to Roosevelt's WPA nurseries, to defense industry centers in World War II, to Head Start during the War on Poverty, the focus of government-sponsored child care programs has been on income maintenance for the poor and—in collaboration with industry—control over female employment in peacetime and wartime economies. While most people might agree that income maintenance for the poor is a rational social priority, as we saw in Chapter 1, the work and family situation of women and mothers has changed dramatically since the late 1960s so as to increase the need for child care services among all social classes.

Regardless of the ubiquity of the "motherhood mandate" calling for the mother's continued responsibility for child care, higher rates of employment, divorce, and poverty among women make traditional motherhood increasingly difficult or undesirable for many families. Yet the alternatives available to them are limited both by an absolute shortage of affordable child care programs and by a negative image of those public programs that do exist. As we have seen, the legacy of public-supported child care programs is that they exist, if at all, only in the case of extreme emergency and for "deficient" families. The consequence of the welfare dependency stigma is that it is not likely to produce great advocacy by parents or politicians of extended government involvement in child care—even in the face of severe shortages. On the contrary, the historical legacy of government-sponsored child care in this country is one reason why in the 1980s, I believe, we are turning instead toward employers to provide the child care support we now need.

1980s: THE NEW ROLE OF EMPLOYERS

In the face of the reality that family life has changed and that working mothers are here to stay, members of government recognize that they have a social obligation to do something about child care. But the social welfare backlash popular in the current period limits interest in extending or providing new public services. Indeed, the drastic cuts in public child care spending since 1981 are rationalized by invoking the historical stigma of government programs discussed throughout this chapter. That is, government programs were to exist as short term, remedial solutions to the problems of the poorest and most dependent in our society. In the current mind-set, their persistence over the years has let people buy into the cycle of government dependency abhorrent to a socially conservative administration.

The child care policies of the Reagan administration since 1981 can be characterized as "combining cutback, decentralization, deregulation, and privatization" (Kahn and Kamerman 1987:23). First, federal programs, aside from Head Start, not only have been cut back but are now virtually nonexistent.

Second, decentralization has been accomplished to some degree by the transformation of Title XX into social service block grants administered to the states for various social services, including child care. The use of these grants is at the discretion of the states, that is, not all states apply them to child care. Consequently, there is great variation in child care delivery and funding among the states. Indeed, few states have a coherent and consistent statewide child care policy (Blank and Wilkins 1985). (The few states that have initiated "workfare" programs—such as New York, Massachusetts, and California—are recognizing the need to provide child care as part of their attempts to get young, low income women off welfare and into the labor market, and some are currently developing pilot services.)

Third, deregulation of public-supported child care was also accomplished by the transformation of Title XX into Social Security block grants, in that proposed minimum standards for federally subsidized programs were eliminated (Kahn and Kamerman 1987). As a result, the states have a wide range of regulatory policies; and, out of concern for cost cutting, most have cut monitoring and enforcement of standards they previously performed.

And finally, in light of the growing need for child care among the not-so-poor, and given the desire to decrease rather than increase government dependency, renewed emphasis is placed on the private sector to be the provider of last resort of social services and benefits, including child care. Privatization of child care is occurring on two levels. One is the growth in the proportion of proprietary child care programs relative to public ones. Private child care chains—such as Kinder Care, La Petite Academe, and Living and Learning—for-profit centers, and individuals providing care for pay have increased their market presence, while public and nonprofit programs have decreased theirs (Kahn and Kamerman 1987).

Second, privatization is occurring through increased government pressure on employers to provide child care benefits to their employees. To shift responsibility for child care from government to employers, the Reagan administration, as part of its White House Private Sector Initiatives program, established a series of meetings and conferences in different states attended by government officials, company chief executive officers, and community leaders. Although little in the way of concrete programs came out of these meetings, they did represent the first step toward creating the kind of public-private partnerships the administration encourages. Indeed, some funds have been provided by the Department of Health and Human Services to "encourage the development of employer-sponsored child care services and related activities" (Kahn and Kamerman 1987:193).

But the most significant incentive provided by government for private, employer-supported child care came with two particular changes in the tax law: the creation of the Dependent Care Assistance Plan (Internal Revenue Code sec. 129), which enables employers to offer child care as a tax-free benefit to employees, and the allowance for flexible benefit packages (Internal Revenue Code sec. 401[k]) in which child care can be one option. (These tax-based incentives are discussed in greater detail in Chapter 3.) It is important to note here that changes introduced by the passage of the 1986 Tax Reform Act—for example, placing new limits on employees' tax-free benefits contributions—may undermine much of the attraction of these programs.

In short, while in his State of the Union address in 1984 President Reagan briefly mentioned that Congress should pass legislation that would encourage employers to become more constructively involved with their employees' child care problems, pressure from him has not gone beyond rhetoric, and Congress has enacted no new legislation to provide employers with further incentives.

CONCLUSION

The historical stigma of government-sponsored child care programs is powerful. Although the association of child care need with economic disadvantage or familial dysfunction clearly does not fit the real situation of a majority of working families, it is a difficult association to shed.

Because government has been, and still is, unwilling to provide child care services to a majority of families who need them, because most parents would prefer child care support to be an employee benefit rather than a government social service, and because employers may be the only segment of society with both the capital and possibly the incentive necessary to establish new programs, increased attention is being paid to the role of employers in providing child care assistance to working parents.

But while it is clear that child care is a prime concern of parents, children, and, to some degree, government—and one for which the supply of services does not nearly fit the need—it remains to be seen under what conditions employers do recognize and assume some responsibility for it. This is the subject of Part II.

NOTES

1. There is no consensus on the exact number of children served under the Lanham program. Government sources claim that as many as 1.6 million children were enrolled, but child care analysts maintain that this number is highly inflated. Steiner (1976) asserts the correct number is 105,000; S. Hartmann (1982) suggests it is 130,000; and Kerr (1973) says it is 600,000. There is no independent way to verify these figures. I cite Kerr's figure because it is about halfway between the low and high estimates.

2. It is important to note that after 1947, women's employment rose again. By 1950, 28.6 percent of all adult women (18.5 million) were in the labor force, constituting nearly 30 percent of all workers (S. Hartmann 1982).

3. Other fine discussions of the assumed temporary nature of female employment during the war are in Rupp (1978:139–157); and S. Hartmann (1982:55–56).

4. Honey suggests that this parallels general sociological findings about the relationship between class and child care attitudes: Working class parents are usually more resistant to public, group programs than are middle or upper class parents.

5. This was equal pay for men and women doing the same job. But there were great differences in pay between traditionally "female" jobs, where most women were still concentrated, and higher paying traditionally "male" jobs. The equal pay policies did not account for the generally sex-segregated labor market (Anderson 1981; Hartmann 1982; Milkman 1987).

PART 2

A LOOK AT
EMPLOYER-SUPPORTED
CHILD CARE

Chapter 3

What Is Employer-Supported Child Care?

Employer-supported child care refers to a situation in which "an employer, group of employers, or a labor union takes some initiative in meeting employees' child care needs and bears some or all of the cost" (Governor's Advisory Committee 1981:4). This rather broad definition covers several types of programs that will be described in this chapter.

THE NUMBERS

The first in-depth survey of employer-supported child care, conducted by the National Employer Supported Child Care Project (NESCCP), identified 415 employers involved in child care support in 1981–1982.[1] By 1985, the Conference Board's Work and Family Information Center estimated that the number of employers supporting child care had risen to 1,850. Table 3.1 shows the distribution of employers by the type of program offered.

Even more recently, informal estimates made by child care advocates put the number of employers supporting child care at 2,500 to 3,000. But it is important to note that all of these numbers are only estimates, as no one has been able to provide an actual list of employers involved in child care, and there has been no systematic, national study comparable with NESCCP's 1981–1982 study to reveal the particular nature of employers' support.

In any event, the NESCCP study, the Conference Board's

TABLE 3.1
**Estimated Number of Employers Supporting Different Types of
Child Care, 1985**

Type of Child Care	Number of Companies
Direct Services	
On- or Off-site Centers	550
Family Day Care	30
After School Care	50
Sick Child Care	20
Information and Referral	300
Financial Assistance	
Vouchers	25
Vendors	300
Flexible Benefits	
Cafeteria Plan	75
Flexible Spending Account/	
Salary Reduction	500
Total	1,850

Source: The Conference Board (1985).

updated estimate, and other research do reveal that most employer-supported child care programs were established quite
recently. For example, of the 261 NESCCP programs on which
there were data, only 40 existed before 1970. In fact, fully one-
third (87) of the programs were established after 1980, sug-
gesting a new surge in employer-supported child care. This surge
corresponds to the tremendous growth in the labor force participation of women with young children (described in Chapter
1), as well as to particular changes in the tax laws that made it
expedient for employers to become more actively involved in
providing child care services.[2] But before we examine the rea-

sons for the recent surge in employer-supported child care, let us look at the types of programs employers provide.

TYPES OF PROGRAMS

There are four general categories of employer-supported child care programs: direct services, information, financial assistance, and alternative work schedules. Within each of these are a number of options that are described below. Some of the advantages and disadvantages of each program, from the perspectives of employers and employee-parents, are noted.

Direct Services

Direct services provide actual child care spaces. The most common direct services are on- or off-site centers, consortium centers, family day care networks, school programs, and summer camps.

Child Care Centers Many companies opt to set up child care centers on or near the work site because of the convenience to parents and/or because they have existing facilities that can easily be converted. However it is done, the establishment of a company center is one of the most expensive options for employers, but one that gives them maximum control.

According to the Conference Board (1985), there were about 550 employers supporting some type of child care center in 1984–1985. The majority of these were health and medical services, which have very high rates of female employment, irregular employment shifts, and particular needs to retain a skilled staff (nurses).

Employer-supported child care centers take many forms. In some companies, the center is a separate department or subsidiary of the company and all child care staff are considered company employees. In others, an outside contractor is hired to design and administer the program. Often, the center is established as a nonprofit corporation with company officials and community members constituting the board of directors. And in some cases, the center is a for-profit subsidiary of the company.

The financial contribution of employers to their child care centers varies. Some choose to contribute only start-up expenses, and others pay ongoing operating expenses—both of which range tremendously. In Magid's (1983) survey, employers reported start-up costs from $300 to $999,999. Hewitt Associates (1982), on the other hand, estimated the range to be $25,000 to $150,000 for centers with 25 to 75 children (a fairly average size).

Ongoing expenses vary even more. Some employers provide space, utilities, and services—such as clerical, administrative, and maintenance—on an ongoing basis. Others contribute a specific portion of costs; and still others pay a fixed dollar amount per child per week, usually working out to be about 50 percent of total costs (J. Auerbach 1986). The bulk of operating expenses—salaries, food, and equipment—in most cases comes out of parent fees. It is estimated that the operating costs of an on-site center is $2,000 to $3,000 per child per year (Magid 1983).

Virtually no employer-supported child care center is free to employees, and the fees parents pay vary a great deal. Some centers charge fees comparable with those of proprietary programs in the surrounding community, while others charge much less. Some receive Title XX subsidies to accommodate low-income families. Additionally, the fee in one center may vary for different age children—infant care is usually more expensive—and between employees and non-employees—employees usually pay a lower rate.

One study found a range of parent fees from $100 to $405 per month per child, with an average of $214, among 16 employer-supported child care centers. In one center, the fee for infant care ($405) was nearly twice that for preschool care ($206), reflecting the smaller staff/child ratio and the greater intensity of infant care (J. Auerbach 1986).

The size of on- and off-site centers range from about 10 to 300 children (Burud et al. 1984). Many centers accept only employees' children, but some also accept children from the surrounding community. This decision is often based on the ability of an employer to fill its child care center with its own employees' children, its first preference. If there is a surplus of spaces, then other children are admitted. The age of children cared for ranges from 6 weeks to 15 years, although most centers offer care only for toddlers and preschoolers.

To my knowledge, all identified employer-supported child care centers observe or better existing state regulations about staff/child ratios. These ratios are always lower for infant care (averaging 1:5) than for toddlers (1:6) and preschoolers (1:13).[3]

Additionally, there is some evidence that employer-supported child care centers tend to hire very highly qualified staffs. Usually child care in both the public and the private sector is a notoriously low paying and unorganized occupation.[4] This has served as a disincentive for many highly educated people to enter the field, and it has called into question the quality of care offered in many programs.

But in my (J. Auerbach 1986) study of 16 employer-supported programs, a carefully chosen staff was the norm. Nearly all programs had directors with postsecondary educational degrees in child development or early childhood education. Many of the other workers in the centers were students in child development and education programs at nearby colleges or universities, or they already had credentials. According to employers, the wages paid to these workers were in all cases comparable with, if not better than, those of proprietary or public child care workers in their community.[5] Furthermore, in most of the on- and off-site centers, child care workers were considered regular employees; they were paid wages comparable with those of similar level employees elsewhere in the company and received benefits. In some cases the directors of the child care centers were considered supervisors or managers of rank and salary comparable with others elsewhere in the company.

Also interesting is the fact that all of the child care centers in this study had some type of curriculum in their program. Fourteen employers identified their curriculum under the general heading of "child development"; one used the "Palo Alto Schools" curriculum, and one had a Montessori program with separate schools for infants and children. In other words, none of these centers was essentially custodial; a great deal of attention was paid to the educational and social quality of the program. Furthermore, there is no imposition of corporate culture or loyalty in the curriculm of any of these or other employer-supported child care centers. Some people assume that employers would be trying to rear "corporate kiddies" in their programs, to foster a sense of loyalty to the organization among the children, but there is no evidence of this. Children do not sing the corporate anthem or learn about colors and letters from the corporate logo. Rather, the particular identity of the employer-sponsor is usually a benign element of its child care center's curriculum.

There are many highly touted examples of employer-supported child care centers. Two of the earliest successful programs were those of Stride-Rite Corporation—a children's shoe manufacturer in Massachusetts—which opened an on-site center in 1974,[6] and Intermedics—a pacemaker manufacturer in Freeport, Texas—which opened its on-site center in 1979. Since then, on- and near-site child care centers have been established by such companies as Wang Laboratories, First Atlanta Corporation, Zale Corporation, Syntex, American Savings and Loan, SAS Institute, and Corning Glass Works, and at many medical facilities, including Sioux Valley Hospital (Iowa), Immanuel Medical Center (Nebraska), St. Dominic's Hospital (Mississippi), and St. Francis Hospital and Medical Center (Connecticut).

Additionally, in some downtown areas and suburban industrial parks, a group of employers together—as a consortium—sponsor a child care center centrally located and made available to each sponsor's employees. In some communities, the developers of industrial parks are constructing child care centers to attract new businesses.

One such center, with room for over 200 children ranging from infants to preschoolers, opened in the fall of 1986 in the Hacienda Business Park in Pleasanton, California (an East Bay community). Its clients are children of employees of such corporate giants as AT&T and Prudential Insurance and of the developer Callahan, Sweeney & O'Brien. Similarly, Trammell Crow Company, one of the largest developers in the nation, opened a child care center in 1985 in an industrial park it owns in West Dallas, Texas.[7]

Finally, some unions have operated child care centers for their membership. The most notable example is the Amalgamated Clothing and Textile Workers Union, which at one time sponsored six centers in the Mid-Atlantic region of the United States. Decline in the apparel industry resulted in the closing of most of these centers by 1983. Other short-lived child care centers were sponsored by the Seafarers International Union in Ponce, Puerto Rico, and the United Federation of Teachers, Local 2, in New York City in the 1970s. These, too, closed because of financial difficulties (Creque 1979).

Currently, in New York City the International Ladies Garment Workers Union is working with public and private funding to support a community child care center for low income employees and union members working in the garment industry in the city's Chinatown district.[8]

The greatest advantage of child care centers to employers is their high visibility, affording the companies recruitment, retention, employee morale, and public relations benefits. (This is discussed further in Chapter 4.) Furthermore, in a center, companies have greater control in ensuring the quality of child care they offer employees. The disadvantages of providing a child care center are primarily the high cost and increased liability.

From the employees' perspective, a company-sponsored child care center on or off the work site may be the best option imaginable because of its convenience, cost, and reliability. But this is true only if the center provides the type of care they need. Many centers don't offer infant or after school care, many have hours of operation incompatible with certain employees' shifts, and many are too expensive for low wage employees. Furthermore, if the employee commutes to a downtown location, often she or he does not want to commute with children to an on- or near-site center. This employee might prefer a center or other option nearer home. Nevertheless, the existence of an on- or near-site company-sponsored center has provided many employee-parents with child care that was otherwise unavailable or inconvenient.

Family Day Care A second type of direct child care service provided by employers is support for family day care, a system in which individuals (in some cases small business people) provide child care in their own homes.[9] This kind of child care is the most common arrangement used by parents in the United States (Chapter 2).

Employers either bring existing providers together into a network that is made available to their employees, or they help establish new providers to whom they refer employees. Employers' support may be financial; they may contribute to their employees' cost of using family day care, or they may contribute money or services directly to the providers. Some employers contribute money to nonprofit community child care agencies that use it to train and establish new family day care providers.

Currently, very few employers support family day care networks, although there appears to be growing interest in doing so.[10] The NESCCP 1981–1982 study identified only 5 out of 415 employers engaged in such a program—all were health care organizations (Burud et al. 1984). The Conference Board (1985) estimates there were 30 employers (out of 1,850) supporting family day care in 1984–1985.

One nonmedical company that sponsors a significant family day care program is Steelcase Industries, the largest manufacturer of office furniture in the United States, located in Grand Rapids, Michigan. Its program involves a network of 250 family day care providers. The providers are independent small business people who do not have an exclusive arrangement with the company. Rather, they are encouraged to accept employee and community children on an equal basis. The company support involves unifying these already established providers into a network, lending them equipment at no charge, offering them free workshops and training sessions, and acting as mediator for them in small business issues. Steelcase does some recruitment to try to establish new providers. In Michigan, all these providers must be registered. (This is how the company initially located all the network members.) Additionally, Steelcase requires them to carry accident insurance (since they lend them equipment) and to attend at least two workshops a year on such things as taxes and health and safety. (The workshops are on business and safety issues rather than on curriculum.) The company also makes periodic home visits to every provider to whom it makes referrals.

The program serves about 300 children, ages six weeks to teenagers, and is believed by Steelcase to best serve employees' diverse needs and to best support existing community child care programs. The cost to parents is arranged with the specific provider.

To parents, family day care is one of the most desirable forms of extrafamilial child care because it reproduces a family/home setting, is relatively small (usually no more than six children), and is often conveniently located in their neighborhood (Baden and Friedman 1981). Family day care is attractive to employers because it requires little or no start-up expense and no continuous overhead, and it is flexible and can serve employees in different locations. Employers also can feel that by supporting a network of providers who operate as small business people (and have tax advantages as such), they encourage others to enter the field and thereby enhance the supply. To the extent that this happens, parents benefit by having more providers from which to choose.

The primary disadvantage of family day care arrangements to both parents and employers is that they are not very well regulated. Many states do not require licensing or registration of such facilities, and those that do are unable to monitor the homes and providers on a regular basis. However, some employers who support family day care networks, like Steelcase, do require providers to be licensed, and monitor them regularly. At a time when parents are increasingly concerned about the safety of their children in child care settings, this regulation is somewhat reassuring.

After School and Summer Care When we think of child care, we often think of children of preschool age. But many parents need care for older children once the school day is over (and the parents are still at work). Popularly referred to as the latchkey phenomenon, the after school care situation has yet to receive much institutional responses.[11] Few programs—public or private—directly address the needs of school age children, although public school systems have instituted programs in a number of states, including Minnesota, California, and New York (Kahn and Kamerman 1987).

Employers can provide after school care in a number of ways. They can accommodate those age groups in their child care centers or family day care networks by arranging for transportation to and from school. Additionally, some have cooperative arrangements with public and private schools to provide before and after school care at a school site. The Conference Board (1985) estimates that 50 employers were providing some type of after school care in 1984–1985.

Among these, Steelcase Industries and Philip Crosby Associates—a management consulting firm in Florida—accommodate school age children in their information and referral services (a program option described below), and in the case of Steelcase, in its family day care network. American Savings and Loan in Stockton, California, has before and after school care for children up to age ten in its near-site child care center, and it provides transportation for them to and from school.

Summer is also a time when parents need reliable care for school age children—and they need it for the entire day, since the children are not in school. Of course, there are many traditional summer programs—private camps, recreation and parks department programs, summer school, and so on—but many are only part day and assume there is a parent at home to care for children the rest of the day, and many are expensive.

Only a few employers now sponsor summer camps for employees' children. No studies of employer-supported child care have precise data on the number of these. However, the best-publicized summer program is that of Fel-Pro Industries in Skokie, Illinois. This company, a gasket manufacturer, purchased rural property in 1970 and developed it into a summer camp for children aged 6 to 15. The children go to work with their parents and are then transported by the company to and from the camp. Over 300 children participate each summer (Burud et al. 1984).

A few other employers provide summer programs for employees' children in addition to their primary child care service. Philip Crosby, for example, has a broad summer program of camps, skills training programs, civic theater, and special programs at community colleges for children up to age 15. In addition, at least a couple of hospitals run summer programs for children up to age 11 or 12 in their on-site child care centers (J. Auerbach 1986).

While a great deal more summer care is needed, these programs provide child care assistance during an otherwise difficult period for working parents.

Information

The second major category of employer-supported child care is information, which generally takes three forms: information (also called resource) and referral services, employee assistance programs, and parent education.

Information and Referral In a 1975 national child care consumer study, parents surveyed about their needs said they would most like government to provide an information and referral system (Friedman 1983a). Over ten years later, little has happened from government in this regard, but many local communities have established nonprofit child care coordinating councils (4Cs) and referral agencies that receive some public funds. In addition, many private organizations have established for-profit information and referral businesses.

Parents are still in great need of information about just what is available in their communities, how to choose a provider, and what rights they and their children have to protect them in different child care situations.

Employers are becoming increasingly active in addressing that concern by providing information and referral services to their employees. Some companies have a service at the work site and employ a person to run it as part of the company. Others contract with local child care agencies—especially the 4Cs—that already have established networks of providers (usually licensed ones only).

Information and referral services are relatively inexpensive to employers and assist them in addressing a broad range of employee needs. They are therefore seen by many employers as more equitable than an on-site center, for example, which serves a more limited population in a more limited setting (Baden and Friedman 1981). This has made information and referral attractive to both large and small companies. A large organization with many locations can establish a corporationwide information and referral service more easily, more equitably, and at much less cost than it can set up a number of child care centers in different states. In a small company, each employee-parent may have a different child care need that cannot be addressed by one type of direct child care service (a center, for example). The ability to make individualized arrangements is preferable for both the parents and the employer.

NESCCP identified 36 employers providing information and referral in 1981–1982 (Burud et al. 1984). By 1985, the Conference Board estimated that number was up to 300.

One example of a large-scale information and referral program is that offered by IBM. Working with a private child care consulting firm called Work/Family Directions, IBM has developed a nationwide network of over 150 community resource and referral agencies to help its employees in different locations . The company has published a booklet that spells out the program, raises questions for parents to consider when choosing a particular provider, and lists telephone numbers to call for assistance in different states and cities.

On a smaller scale, Philip Crosby Associates contracts with the local Florida 4Cs to provide information and referral services to its employees. Representatives from the 4Cs meet individually with employees to help them determine what kind of program they want and where to find it. The company pays half of the charges to parents—up to $25 per week—regardless of the type of child care program, provided that program is approved by the 4Cs. The service accommodates children aged 6 weeks to 15 years. A representative from the 4Cs comes to the company regularly to discuss the fit between employees' needs and the service it is providing. Additionally, the 4Cs acts as a monitor for parents, checking up on children's attendance at various programs.

Philip Crosby Associates is a relatively small company (175 employees in 1985). Ten to 12 percent of employees have children in child care programs referred by the 4Cs, which represents 80 percent of eligible families. In this case, the diversity of need (as well as the perceived cost of an on-site center) drove the company to establish an information and referral service.

Other companies offering information and referral services to their employees include 3M, Steelcase (in addition to its family day care network), McDonalds, Kraft Foods, American Express, Equitable Life, and Time.

In large and small companies alike, access to information and referral to established providers is a great help to parents and supports existing community child care resources. Some employers and advocates argue that employer support of information and referral services in fact helps to increase the supply and improve the quality of child care in a community by making demand better known (Baden and Friedman 1981).

Employee Assistance Programs Some employers become aware of child care problems and needs among their employees through the existence of employee assistance programs (EAP).[12] These are usually counseling-type services located in personnel or human resource departments. Employees are encouraged to talk with a counselor about problems in their family or personal life that may affect their work performance, such as alcoholism, drug abuse, or marital discord.

Increasingly, child care is also a real problem for employees. As concern about what is happening with one's children during the day translates into distraction, tardiness, or absenteeism, it becomes a problem for employers. Minimizing those occurrences may allow an employer to recoup the cost of an EAP through reduced turnover and benefits costs.

While an EAP exists primarily as a way for employees to relieve some of their stress by talking with a counselor, it can sometimes lead to the direct implementation of an employer-supported child care program. This was the case at 3M, where the increased expression of child care problems led to the establishment of an in-house information and referral service.

Parent Education Many employers consider parent education to be a type of child care assistance. Certainly, some working parents find that rearing children in this complex world requires some guidance. Working mothers, in particular, want accurate information about just how much of an effect their absence during the day has on their children. Many women still experience guilt about leaving their young children to the care of others. They are aware of conflicting arguments and research about just what children need from their mothers as they develop. (Interestingly, this question has not been raised about men.)

Divorce, family separation, and remarriage also produce anxiety and conflict between parents and children. Furthermore, with increased awareness of child abuse and greater advocacy of children's rights in the society at large, many parents are confused about how to relate to their children. Parent education programs exist to address these questions and concerns.

Employers who provide parent education do so primarily to reduce family-related stress that spills over into the work performance of their employees. The advantage to them—and to employees—is that the information and support garnered from such a program can help employees learn coping strategies and be less distracted at work. Additionally, in offering parent education, employers appear concerned about their employees, which contributes to good public relations (Baden and Friedman 1981). And, on the whole, it is a very inexpensive program.

The Conference Board (1985) estimates that 500 to 1,000 employers provided parent education 1984–1985. The services generally include noon-time seminars with guest speakers, workshops on particular topics, and newsletters with information and tips on parenting.

In sum, information is in many ways as difficult for working parents to access—and as important—as actual child care services. Establishing information and referral, employee assistance, and parent education programs are ways in which employers are helping. Although these programs do nothing directly to increase the actual supply of child care in a community, they do constitute one significant type of employer support.

Financial Assistance

A third general category of employer-supported child care is financial assistance. The form of financial support varies among

employers and is affected—like other program—by the size of
the company, its service or product, the extent and nature of
parent need, cost, and existing community resources. Types of
financial assistance include vendor arrangements, vouchers,
flexible benefits, and corporate contributions to existing child
care agencies and programs.

Vendor Arrangements In a vendor program, an employer ar-
ranges for a discounted rate for employees using an existing
local, licensed child care center. Often in a vendor program,
the employer purchases a number of enrollment spaces at a
discounted fee for use by its employees. Usually, the discount
is about 10 percent of the fees to give parents a total 20 percent
reduction.

In some cases, employers pay the portion of fees parents cannot afford, or the portion not paid by public sources for eligible employees (Title XX primarily), and use the local 4Cs as a
broker between all parties involved.

It is common to find vendor arrangements between employers and national proprietary child care chains, such as Kinder
Care, Children's World, and La Petite Academe, because the
arrangement is beneficial to both.[13] For the employer, who is
paying only 10 percent and may have only a few employees
enrolled in the center, the discount is relatively inexpensive. At
the same time, a vendor program assists the chain operators in
filling unused spaces, and it enhances their marketing abilities
through increased publicity among employees. Friedman (1985)
estimates that there are about 300 employers contracting with
a for-profit chain of child care centers.

Vendor programs are available almost exclusively from proprietary programs because they have more operating flexibility
than nonprofit centers and are better able to reduce fees. Also,
they can offer an unlimited number of spaces to any one employer, while nonprofit centers cannot show favoritism (Friedman 1985).

Employees benefit from reduced child care costs in a vendor
arrangement, but they are limited to using a particular program that may not suit their specific child care needs. Child
care chains, like Kinder Care, usually have one location in a
city or suburb that may be very inconvenient for many parents.

Furthermore, many parents do not like the idea of franchise child care, believing it is too uniform, too rigid, and unable to provide the individualized programs they would prefer. (Franchise child care has popularly been referred to as "Kentucky Fried Children"!)

Interestingly, some employers who had a vendor arrangement with one of these child care chains are now seeking alternatives. For example, Equitable Life, which contracted with Kinder Care in three states, found that the sites were inconvenient and that employees were not participating at the rate anticipated. Consequently, the company decided to develop an information and referral service instead.

Vouchers Vouchers are a way of subsidizing child care expenses incurred by employees, and they operate essentially like a credit. Usually employers contribute a portion of the total of an employee's child care costs, and will pay only for care provided in a licensed center or family day care home. (Polaroid pays for care by relatives, too.) Payments may be made either to the employee or to the provider. A system of direct payment may be arranged with a local public 4Cs or agency.

Two of the most publicized child care voucher programs are those of Polaroid Corporation in Cambridge, Massachusetts, and the Ford Foundation in New York City. Both of these companies, however, provide vouchers only for employees in lower income categories. The amount of the voucher varies according to need, but the maximum in both companies is 50 percent of child care costs.

The advantage to employers in providing a child care voucher is that it maximizes parent choice. The employer is allowing parents to choose their provider within certain limits (a licensed program). The main disadvantage of a voucher program for employers is that it is expensive. The amount of subsidy must be substantial for the parents to experience any meaningful reduction in child care costs.

The disadvantage for parents is that voucher does not contribute to the actual supply of child care, although it does give them flexibility in choosing from what is available in licensed care (Polaroid's voucher for care by relatives notwithstanding). The Conference Board (1985) estimates only 25 employers provided child care vouchers in 1984–1985, and others have predicted that this form of employer support will not proliferate, primarily because of its cost (Friedman 1985).

Flexible Benefits Many people in the child care field believe that flexible benefits packages may be the wave of the future in employer-supported child care because they address two fundamental problems that arise in other options: cost and equity (see especially Friedman 1985). As already mentioned, direct employer-supported child care is expensive. It also is not something that appeals to all workers: Only a small portion of any one work force is of childbearing age, and therefore likely to take advantage of it at any one time. Directly sponsoring child care therefore raises the question of equity for employers who feel pressured to initiate additional programs with broader appeal. For these two reasons—cost and equity—child care as a flexible benefit option has become increasingly attractive to employers.

With the passage of Internal Revenue Code sec. 125 in 1978, child care can be included as part of an existing flexible benefits program—usually a cafeteria plan.[14] A cafeteria plan must have a core coverage (usually medical, dental, and disability insurance, vacation, and retirement) and an allowance of flexible credits to use in putting together an individual's plan around the core.

The most common form of child care as a flexible benefit is a reimbursement applied under a dependent care assistance program (DCAP) set up by the employer (Internal Revenue Code sec. 129). This enables employers to offer child care as a tax-free benefit to employees. The DCAP may take three forms: (1) if there is an on-site center, the employer pays for it; (2) an employer pays dependent care costs directly to the provider of parents' choice; and (3) an employer reimburses the employee for the cost of care.

The regulations surrounding DCAPs illustrate their intent. For an employer to establish a DCAP, it must prepare a written plan and disseminate it to all employees. It cannot discriminate, nor can more than 25 percent of the amount paid by the employer for child care be paid on behalf of a group of persons each of whom owns more than 5 percent of the profits or capital interest in an unincorporated employer. Additionally, the amount of the benefit offered an employee as nontaxable is limited to an amount equal to the earned income of an unmarried employee or, if the employee is married, the earned income of the spouse with the lower earnings, even if that spouse is not employed. An unemployed spouse who is a student or is disabled is assumed ţo have earned $200 per month if there is one child or $400 per month if there are two or more children. An employee with any other nonworking spouse (i.e., one who is neither a student nor disabled), will have to pay taxes on the value of any child care benefit received from the employer (Friedman 1985). Obviously, then, this plan is intended to aid families in which there is no one available during the day to care for children.

A second type of flexible benefits approach is a salary reduction, usually in the form of a flexible spending account (FSA). Under this program, employees set up an account for expenses, such as child care, not covered by a regular benefits package. Pretax money is contributed from the employee's salary into the FSA.[15] Employers ususally place a cap on the amount of reduction to avoid discriminatory practices.[16]

While between 300 and 500 companies have set up FSAs, there is little utilization of this option for child care. This may be due in part to recent changes in the rules governing FSAs. Since 1984, the IRS has ruled that (1) employees must make an irrevocable selection of benefits once a year and they must elect the amount *before* the actual expense is incurred; (2) benefits elections may be reduced with a change in status, such as marriage, divorce, adoption of a child, or termination of employment; and (3) all unused funds are forfeited (Friedman 1985).

Three major corporations that have dependent/child care as an option in their flexible benefits plans are American Can, Procter and Gamble, and Educational Testing Service. Both American Can and Procter and Gamble, however restrict eligibility for flexible benefits to certain salaried employees (see Friedman 1985:22–23 for more details).

Companies that have FSAs, primarily salary reduction plans, include Chemical Bank, Hewitt Associates, Mellon Bank, and PepsiCo. The funds in the accounts established for child care

are either disbursed in their employees' regular paychecks or in separate periodic payments (Friedman 1985).

Child care as a flexible benefit option has advantages and disadvantages for both employers and employees. It is advantageous to employers because, in the first place, it requires little or no additional outlay of money. In fact, according to analysts, it has the potential to be cost saving. Benefit programs are usually designed with an "average" employee in mind—a male breadwinner. But he represents an increasingly smaller percent of the actual work force.[17] Additionally, many families now have two wage earners who receive essentially duplicate benefits. Thus, some of the benefits in a standardized plan go to waste. Flexible plans help control costs because benefits are allocated only to those employees who choose them.

A second advantage to employers is that because child care is only one option in a flexible benefit package, people can choose others, thereby avoiding the equity problem. And finally, as a form of employer-supported child care, the flexible benefit program maximizes parental choice in determining the nature of care their children receive.

But child care as a flexible benefit option does have some disadvantages for both employers and employees. First, as a tax-tied benefit, it is subject to changes in tax codes, which threatens its stabililty. Second, from the employer's end, keeping track of all the individualized plans of the employees requires sophisticated data processing that is laborious if not costly. (Of course, the employer may decide that the benefit of such a program far outweighs the troublesomeness of administering it.) And finally, in relation to other forms of employer-supported child care, the benefit option does not actually increase the number of available child care slots, and is therefore disadvantageous to those concerned with the bottom line of supply.

It also is important to stress that a large number of American employees are not covered by benefits programs, particularly those employees who earn low incomes, work part-time, work irregularly, and are not protected by a union. Many of these employees are precisely those who most need child care assistance. Incorporating child care into a company's flexible benefits program available only to salaried employees (as in the cases of Procter and Gamble and American Can) would not do these employees any good, and might contribute to the further stratification of availability of child care resources between high income and low income parents.

Corporate Contributions Employers may choose to take a financial approach to solving child care problems that is not limited to assisting their own employees. Some contribute money directly to existing child care programs, some contribute to child care agencies (such as the 4Cs) to encourage the expansion of existing programs as well as the development of new ones in their community, and others use their corporate standing to encourage other employers and foundations to make contributions to a community child care fund (usually administered by a public child care agency).

The Conference Board (1985) estimates there are between 500 and 1,000 employers who support child care through corporate contributions of one of these kinds. Usually, the employees of a contributing company are not guaranteed enrollment in any particular child care program, but it is assumed that they benefit from having an enhanced supply available in their community.

John Hancock Mutual Life Insurance is one company that has been making significant financial contributions for child care since 1981. Hancock contributes to United Way of Massachusetts Bay for explicit use for child care and it supports two nonprofit child care centers in Boston.

In a couple of states, employers contribute financial assistance to public-private child care funds. In Texas, for example, over 40 corporations contribute to the Corporate Child Development Fund, which allocates money to child care programs in rural and low income areas. This fund was conceived and initiated by the Levi Strauss Foundation and the state's Department of Human Resources in 1979 as a "public-private partnership,"[18] and now contributes to over 30 community-based child care programs serving over 3,000 children.

A similar public-private partnership, the California Child Care Initiative, was established in California in 1984. Primary financial backing came from the Bank of America Foundation, which made an initial $100,000 contribution and then used corporate leveraging to solicit similar contributions from major companies, foundations, and local governments. The money collected is used to support the existing statewide child care resource and referral network, but the long term plan is to use some of the money to train and establish new providers in a variety of settings—child care centers as well as family day care homes. The emphasis is on enhancing the quality and supply of community based child care.

Besides the Bank of America Foundation, corporate contributors include Chevron USA, Inc., Pacific Gas and Electric Company, Clorox Company Foundation, Mervyn's, McKesson, and Pacific Telesis Foundation. In addition, the Contra Costa Board of Supervisors and the City and County of San Francisco contributed public money. Once again, while the employees of any one of these sponsors are not guaranteed placement in a program, it is assumed that they will benefit from the increased supply in their communities.

With its wide variety of options, financial assistance is an increasingly attractive form of employer-supported child care. Within this category, flexible benefits are emerging as the most popular option for employers (Friedman 1985). Indeed, in *Families at Work: Strengths and Strains* (General Mills 1981), 70 percent of the corporate human resources officers surveyed responded that their company was most likely to adopt some type of flexible benefits program over the next five years. A flexible benefits program is so popular because it best addresses the wide range of needs among a diversified work force, and it does so at relatively little expense to the employer.

On the other hand, a child care voucher might be the most attractive financial option to parents because it is a direct money subsidy and can be applied to their provider of choice. But because it represents the greatest financial commitment of all the options, a voucher is the least popular option among most employers (Friedman 1985).

Whatever compromise is reached between employers' and employees' preferences, financial assistance will probably be the most rapidly growing employer option because it serves a greater number of working parents with a variety of child care needs. Whether it will contribute in any way to increasing the actual supply of child care services is still unclear.

Alternative Work Schedules

Alternatives to the normal nine to five, five days-a-week work schedule are becoming increasingly desirable to employees in their attempts to balance work and family life. Employers offering alternative work schedules argue that they are at least indirectly supporting child care by making it possible for parents to care for their children at home much of the time and to better accommodate the hours of operation of local child care centers and homes. Alternative scheduling options include flex-time, part-time, job sharing, and flexible parental leaves.

Flex-time, Part-time, and Job sharing Flex-time, part time, and job sharing may reduce the amount of extrafamilial child care a family needs, but they do not eliminate it altogether. Flex-time, in which an employee works an eight hour day beginning somewhere between 7 AM and 10 AM and ending between 3 PM and 6 PM, or works longer hours on fewer days per week, is helpful to two earner families who experience work-family time conflicts. But it is certainly not a panacea, especially for child care problems (Bohen and Viveros-Long 1981). Whatever shift an employed parent works, she or he must be able to find reliable child care. Furthermore, flex-time usually is not introduced by employers for that purpose. Rather, it is generally established to reduce absenteeism, tardiness, or commuter congestion, and to raise employee morale and productivity (Baden and Friedman 1981), so it doesn't necessarily imply a conscious effort by employers' to accommodate their employees' child care needs. Nevertheless, family members, human resource officers, and labor leaders all agree that flex-time might help employees balance work and family responsibilities better (General Mills 1981).

Part-time work is desirable to many women—if they can afford it—because it allows them time at home during the day to be with their children. It also makes it easier and less costly for them to arrange more informal child care during the time that they are at work. But, according to analysts, part-time work is ultimately just as costly to companies as full-time, so there is little incentive for employers to institutionalize it for a majority of their employees (Baden and Friedman 1981). (Other problems with part-time work will be mentioned in a moment.)

Job sharing is another alternative method of scheduling that has the potential to provide employees time for child care at home. For employers, job sharing can increase efficiency and energy, and give them a better range of skills. But, like part-time work, job sharing is expensive because separate benefits— if benefits exist—must be paid to two employees instead of one. Additionally, there is opposition to job sharing from unions because it is seen as a way for employers to avoid paying overtime (Baden and Friedman 1981). Overall, few employers offer job sharing as a scheduling option.

Flexible Leaves The leave policies that most directly relate to child care are those governing maternity and parental leaves, a policy realm in which the United States lags far behind other developed nations. As Kamerman and Kahn (1981) have pointed out, maternity and parental leaves are addressed in statutory provisions in all advanced industrial societies except the United States. In this country, pregnancy is viewed and treated under the law as a disability. This enables it to qualify as a nondiscriminatory basis for a leave, but it limits the amount of time one can take off.[19] Extended maternity or parental leaves are granted at the discretion of the employer but must be permitted on a nondiscriminatory basis; that is, they must be treated no differently from other types of disability. This makes it difficult for employers to grant a suitable amount of time for maternity/parental leave, relative to other disabilities.

Furthermore, the provisions that employers make range tremendously with regard to the amount of time allowed off with or without pay and the security of resuming one's job and salary upon returning.[20]

One consequence of the overall lack of meaningful maternity leave policies among employers is that it forces many women to return to work sooner than they would choose, and it floods the demand for the limited number of infant care services already in existence. While a number of employers now offer parental leave—where either parent may take time off after a birth to stay home and care for the child—few fathers take advantage of it. Many simply don't want to, and others are concerned that even though the policy exists, it is still frowned upon for a man to appear willing to disrupt his career for family responsibilities. This is true even though in the General Mills (1981) study, when asked about the policy's desirability, 38 percent of working men, 39 percent of working women, and 42 percent of working mothers said that paid personal leave for fathers for paternity would be of "some" or a "great deal" of help in balancing work and family responsibilities.

Alternative work schedules have been discussed only cursorily here because they represent a much more indirect approach to employer-supported child care than other options. The flexibility of schedules and leaves policies is increasing among employers, and it does assist many parents in making their child care arrangements.

Yet there are two problems with treating these policies as a form of child care. First, they do virtually nothing to enhance the supply of child care and, at best, provide a partial solution for some parents. Second, they reinforce the marginality of many women workers. This is especially true of part-time workers.

Eighty percent of all part-time workers in the United States are women, who on the whole have scanty fringe benefits and work in low wage occupations (Lopata et al. 1984). While part-time work may give them more time to care for their children, it does little to improve their financial and occupational opportunities, and instead reinforces the image of women workers as transient and uncommitted.[21] It is therefore not something to encourage uncritically as a form of child care support.

Now that we have a general picture of the different types of employer-supported child care, it is important to discuss who is sponsoring them. While I have already given examples of some specific companies, the question is, Do they fit a particular profile? In other words, are there demographic and organizational characteristics that distinguish employers who do (or are likely to) offer a child care benefit from those who do not? This is an important question to answer because it informs our understanding of the reasons employers get involved in child care (or do not)—the subject of Chapter 4—and our ability to analyze the significance and the future of their involvement.

EMPLOYER CHARACTERISTICS

While there are no comprehensive, national data, there are a number of smaller scale studies that have attempted to determine the characteristics of employers who do provide a child care benefit (Anderson 1983; Burud et al. 1984; Magid 1983; Perry 1980). While all of these studies contribute greatly to our knowledge of employer-supported child care, many do not provide any quantitative data to substantiate general findings. Additionally, most studies have been based only on employers who are already involved.

What has been conspicuously lacking in the research on employer-supported child care are studies that look at both employers who have a child care program (or are actively considering one) and those who do not.[22] This comparison is necessary in order to make any meaningful generalizations and predictions about the nature of employer-supported child care and its likelihood of expanding even further.

Consequently, in the fall of 1986, I conducted a comparative survey of employers who have or are investigating a child care benefit and those who are not interested. The sample of 99 employers, representing companies in different industries, was drawn from the Delaware Valley—an 11 county area encompassing parts of Pennsylvania, New Jersey, and Delaware.[23] I classified the status of employers' involvement in child care as "offering" child care, "investigating" the possibility of doing so, or "neither" offering nor investigating child care. Even though a majority (69) of employers fell into the classification of "neither," I found some interesting differences in the comparisons between those involved and those uninvolved in the provision of child care.

The following overview of employer characteristics is based on this Delaware Valley survey as well as on information I gathered from all published studies of employer supported child care.

TABLE 3.2
Involvement Status by Sex of the Work Force (proportion female)

Proportion Female	Involvement Status		
	Offering	Investigating	Neither
0-49%	25%(3)	17% (2)	52% (33)
50-100%	75% (9)	83% (10)	48% (30)
Total	100% (12)	100% (12)	100% (63)

$N = 87$.
12 missing cases.

Demographic Characteristics

Sex of the Work Force Studies of employer-supported child care suggest that the most significant factor affecting an employer's involvement in child care is the proportion of female workers it has: Most employers who support a child care benefit have large proportions of women in their labor force (Anderson 1983; Burud et al. 1984; Magid 1983).

For example, in the Delaware Valley survey 75 percent of employers who were offering and 83 percent of those who were investigating child care had a work force that was between 50 and 100 percent female. In comparison, only 48 percent of companies that were neither offering nor investigating child care had a work force with this high a proportion of women (Table 3.2).

Since in most cases mothers are still endowed with the responsibility of child care, the organizations that employ them in great numbers will be the ones most likely to recognize and feel a child care problem when it arises. They will therefore be more likely than others to investigate a solution. (The specific reasons for their activity are elaborated in Chapter 4.)

Employment Sector The American labor market is generally still sex segregated, that is, certain occupations and sectors are composed primarily of women and others are composed of men.[24] The sectors most represented among employers supporting child care are those with high rates of female employment in general. These are service (particularly health care), finance (such as banking and insurance), communications, and high technology (Anderson 1983; Burud et al. 1984; Magid 1983).

Health care has long been the major sector in which employer-supported child care programs are found. Seventy-one percent of programs identified by Perry (1978) were those of hospitals and medical centers, as were 52 percent in Magid's (1983) survey a few years later. However, Burud et al. (1984) found a more even distribution of programs between their general categories of "medical" and "industrial" employers (each sector had 47 percent). Since these researchers do not disaggregate the "industrial" category, it is unclear exactly what type of businesses are represented. Nevertheless, in looking at the list provided at the end of their report, one can see that most "industrial" sponsors are in heavily female sectors (Burud et al. 1984:315–343).

In any event, the fact that service, such as medical care, is the fastest growing sector of the economy (O'Connell and Bloom 1987) explains in part the proliferation of employer-supported child care.

Age of Employees It is often difficult to obtain information about employees' ages, either because employers do not keep explicit records (although they can determine their employees' ages from health benefits applications) or because they consider it private information. Nevertheless, some studies have been able to obtain information—in some cases estimates—on employees' ages. And, as one might predict, the average age of employee population affects the likelihood of an employer's involvement in child care.

Indeed, in the Delaware Valley survey, a significant relationship ($p = .05$) was discovered between the two variables. As we see from Table 3.3, an overwhelming majority of employers who were either offering or investigating child care had an employee population whose average age approximated childbear-

TABLE 3.3
Involvement Status by Average Age of Employees

Average Age	Involvement Status		
	Offering	Investigating	Neither
18–35	82% (9)	77% (10)	41% (23)
36–60*	18% (2)	23% (3)	59% (33)
Total	100% (11)	100% (13)	100% (56)

$N = 80$.
19 missing cases.
*No employers had employees with an average age of over 60.

ing age (defined as 18 to 35), compared with only 41 percent of companies with no involvement. Furthermore, the majority of companies that were neither offering nor investigating child care had employees whose average age was between 36 and 60.

Geographic Location Geographic location in and of itself is of little significance in determining which employers support child care. That is, all studies suggest that employer-supported child care is found in almost all states, although there is disagreement about its concentration. Magid (1983), for example, found the greatest concentration of supporters in the Northeast, while Burud et al. (1984) found it to be in the West. Given the absence of comprehensive, national data, it is impossible to know for certain if either is correct.

Nevertheless, what we do know is that the economic climate of a particular geographic area is likely to affect the development of employer-supported child care initiatives. For example, states that currently are experiencing a boom economy as a result of the growth of finance, service, and high technology businesses in their areas—such as California and Massachusetts—seem to have more employer-supported child care activity. Conversely, regions experiencing an economic bust, such as the South, with recent losses in oil and textile industries, are seeing less interest in employer initiatives.

Studies also show that programs are located in all geographic settings—urban, suburban, and rural (Anderson 1983; Magid 1983; Burud et al. 1984). Interestingly, with the proliferation of new service and high technology industrial parks, the suburbs are fast becoming one of the primary locations of consortium-type employer-supported child care programs in particular. As mentioned earlier in this chapter, a number of companies located in such a park cosponsor a child care center on their premises that is made available to employees of all those companies.

Size of the Company Most analysts agree that the size of a company is not an important determinant of whether it will support child care. Indeed, companies of all sizes—from under 100 to over 80,000 employees—offer child care benefits (Anderson 1983; Burud et al. 1984; Magid 1983). The size of a company, however, may affect the type of program an employer chooses to establish, although that decision is also based on other variables, such as location, existing community resources, and the diversity of employees' child care needs (see especially Magid 1983).

Organizational Characteristics

Unionization Perhaps the most significant organizational characteristic that affects interest in child care is whether an employer is unionized. In general, employer-supported child care programs are found in nonunionized organizations. This is because, as mentioned, these programs are found mostly in growth sectors of the labor force that are highly female and traditionally not highly union organized.

Furthermore, it is possible that unionization may be a significant deterrent to an organization's even considering child care. For example, if there is a union, the employer may view it as the union's responsibility to provide a child care benefit out of its collective bargaining fund (something allowable since the 1969 amendment to the Taft-Hartley Act). In this case, the employer might opt to provide only the same basic benefits to nonunion employees as union employees have, and to not consider others, such as child care (Anderson 1983).

There is also speculation that some companies are considering child care as a means of avoiding unionization, although there is little evidence to substantiate this claim (Baden and Friedman 1981).

Whether a deliberate tactic to avoid labor organization or not, employers who have little or no unionization are more likely to offer or consider providing child care than are those with a significant union presence. As we can see from Table 3.4, over three-fourths of the respondents in the Delaware Valley survey who were either offering or invesigating child care and who gave information about unionization had none at all, compared with 52 percent of the employers who were not involved in child care. (Interestingly, a majority of all employers—regardless of child care interest—had no unionized employees, perhaps reflecting the overall decline in union membership in this country.) Conversely, only 2 out of 29 employers (7 percent) offering or investigating child care had work forces that were at least 50 percent unionized, while nearly one-third of employers with no child care involvement had a work force that was at least 50 percent unionized.

Present Benefits Program So far, no study has examined employer-supported child care in relation to an organization's entire benefits program. Often the details of such programs are not made available to the public or to researchers, as they serve a very competitive function between employers. But there is some indication that organizations with relatively generous policies are more likely to consider providing child care. This is particularly true in cases where other family-related programs exist. For example, companies that have employee counseling programs may be more likely to consider child care, since "Employee counseling programs indicate that the organization already has an appreciation for the interactive dynamic between family life and job performance and has demonstrated its willingness to make an investment to improve the situation for their employees" (Anderson 1983:46).

Interest in providing child care seems to exist even more among many employers who are using flexible benefits pack-

TABLE 3.4
Involvement Status by Unionization (proportion employees unionized)

Proportion Unionized	Involvement Status		
	Offering	Investigating	Neither
0%*	79% (11)	80% (12)	52% (36)
1-49%	2% (1)	20% (3)	16% (11)
50-100%	14% (2)	0% (0)	32% (22)
Total	100% (14)	100% (15)	100% (69)

N = 98.
1 missing case.
*A majority of all employers (60.2 percent) had no unionized employees.

ages competitively to attract and retain desirable employees. (Recruitment and retention as motives for employer-supported child care are discussed fully in Chapter 4.) For example, in the Delaware Valley survey a significant positive relationship (p = .001) existed between interest in flexible benefits and involvement in child care among the employers surveyed. Sixty percent of employers offering child care and 80 percent of those investigating it were also offering or considering flexible benefits, while 86 percent of those not involved in child care were not interested in flexible benefits (Table 3.5).

Corporate Philosophy One final characteristic of companies that may play a significant part in their attitude about offering a child care benefit for their employees is their corporate philosophy (or culture). While it is a difficult concept to define, perhaps a useful definition of corporate philosophy is "the 'personality' of the company that sets it apart from others" (Anderson 1983:45). This is an appropriate definition because child care as a benefit is seen as something competitive among employ-

TABLE 3.5
Involvement Status by Interest in Flexible Benefits

Interest in Flexible Benefits	Involvement Status Offering	Investigating	Neither
Offering	40% (6)	20% (3)	7% (5)
Considering	20% (3)	60% (9)	7% (5)
Neither	40% (6)	20% (3)	86% (59)
Total	100% (15)	100% (15)	100% (69)

$N = 99$.

ers—something that sets one apart from another. Furthermore, many employers who do support a child care program explain their involvement as something that "fits" the particular personality or character of their organization.

Many sponsors of child care describe the corporate philosophy of their organizations as "progressive." Included among the various meanings employers attribute to this expression are a willingness to listen to employees' needs; an effort to treat all employees as individuals; an openness to change; and a willingness to take risks.

The other type of philosophy self-identified by employers who support child care may be called family oriented. This exists in many small to medium size family-owned or -operated businesses where family values are reflected in corporate policy (Friedman 1983a). These employers encourage close relationships with their employees and try to keep attuned to what occurs both at work and at home. Rather than taking the position that work life is wholly separate from home life, they acknowledge the indissoluble link between the two. They see their employees not just as workers but as family members—of their own individual families and of the larger company family. These employers take a benevolent approach to providing child care for their employees. It is done, according to them, as a service to help parents balance work and family life.

Furthermore, some larger companies that produce family oriented products might be likely to support child care for their employees, but probably more for public relations purposes than out of concern for their employees. In these companies, Friedman (1983b:8) notes, "Management is genuinely concerned about the way families, as their principal consumers, perceive their commitment to families."

CONCLUSION

Interest in employer-supported child care is most likely among companies that have a high proportion of women; are in the service, finance, or high technology sector; have employees of childbearing age; are in economically sound locations; are non-unionized; offer flexible benefits; and have a relatively "progressive" employment philosophy. This is not to say that these are the only employers who might support a child care program: On the contrary, a number of partially unionized manufacturing companies have instituted effective programs (Anderson 1983; Burud et al. 1984; Friedman 1985). But as a generalization, if there is further growth in employer-supported child care, we can expect it to be greater among employers who approximate the profile drawn here.

Although in earlier years sponsoring child care centers appeared to be the only option for employers wishing to assist their employees, now there is a much broader range of possible involvement. Both the choice of whether to support child care and the determination of what type of program an employer establishes are based on a number of factors, including the size and location of the company, the number of parent-employees in need, the range of those parents' needs, the cost of various options, and the supply of child care in the surrounding community.

Some options are becoming more attractive than others, for example, including child care as a flexible benefit option rather than building an on-site child care center. But only over time and with more evidence about the nature, advantages, and disadvantages of various programs in existence will we know which are more attractive and likely to proliferate, and will our still somewhat vague picture of employer-supported child care become clearer.

In the meantime, now that we do know a bit about who these employers are and what types of child care programs they sponsor, the next question is *why*, exactly, are they becoming involved? Since not all companies that fit the general profile drawn in this chapter do provide a child care benefit, the question is why some and not others? What explanations are given by officials within organizations for their decision to provide what is still a fairly unusual—but increasingly necessary—benefit to working parents? And what do these tell us about the likelihood of expansion in employer-supported child care and its relation to women's employment? These questions are addressed in the following chapter.

NOTES

1. Earlier studies were conducted by Stein (1973) and Perry (1978); however, Stein's was less systematic and Perry's looked only at centers.

2. Although there were a few earlier programs, it was in the 1970s, as women began reentering the labor force in great numbers, that employer-supported child care emerged as a real possibility, prompted particularly by changes in tax laws. The Revenue Act of 1971, for example, included a provision permitting businesses to deduct at an accelerated capital investment rate the expense of "acquiring, constructing, reconstructing or rehabilitating property for use as a child care facility." (This provision was later amended with the accelerated cost recovery system of depreciation for property placed in child care service after 1980—Internal Revenue Code sec. 168.) Additional modifications in the tax codes allowed employers to deduct any expenses of providing child care that could be considered "ordinary and necessary" business expenses (for example, medical insurance for a child care center at the work site). For more details on these laws, see Commerce Clearing House (1982).

3. These averages were calculated from state by state data collected by the Children's Defense Fund (Blank and Wilkins 1985).

4. Grubb and Lazerson (1982) note how resistance to professionalizing child care workers keeps the occupation low status and low pay.

5. Few employers reported the actual wages paid to their child care workers, but all implied that they were at least comparable with similar workers' elsewhere. Most had studied the wage scales of child care workers in their community as a basis for determining their own.

6. For details on Stride-Rite's child care center, see Judith Brown Kamm,"Stride-Rite's Children's Center, Inc." (Boston: Institute for Case Development and Research, Graduate School of Management, Simmons College, 1975).

7. For descriptive accounts of these consortium programs, see *Dallas Morning News,* Sept. 14, 1986:18K; *San Francisco Chronicle,* Sept. 11, 1986:6.

8. For more on the role of unions in supporting child care, see the appendix to this volume.

9. For a complete discussion of family day care, see Kahn and Kamerman (1987, esp. Ch. 7).

10. Policy experts like Kahn and Kamerman (1987) recommend that family day care be a significant component of all child care planning, including employer-supported child care.

11. For a complete discussion of school age child care, see Baden et al. (1982).

12. For more general discussions of employee assistance programs, see William J. Sonnenstuhl, *Strategies for Employee Assistance Programs: The Crucial Balance* (Ithaca, NY: ILR Press, New York State School of Industrial and Labor Relations, Cornell University, 1986); and Walter F. Scanlon, *Alcoholism and Drug Abuse in the Workplace: Employee Assistance Programs* (New York: Praeger, 1986).

13. There are at present a few national for-profit child care chains, most notably Kinder Care, which operated over 500 centers serving 53,000 children in 1985. Others with a significant market share are Children's World and La Petite Academy. While many employers and parents like the known element of a franchise, many do not. Employers I interviewed (J. Auerbach 1986) often juxtaposed the quality of their program with the perceived lack of quality of Kinder Care or other franchises—especially with regard to their ability to accommodate the individual needs of children. These employers felt that if the franchises are making a profit, they must be skimping somewhere. Nevertheless, it is the franchises that are often in the best position to accommodate employers who want to establish a vendor program.

14. For more details of how flexible benefit plans work, see Howard Fine,"Flexible/Cafeteria Plans," in Jeffrey D. Mamorsky (ed.), *Employee*

Benefits Handbook, 1985 Update (Boston: Warren, Gorham & Lamont, 1985).

15. With the passage of the Tax Reform Act of 1986, new limits have been set on employees' tax-free benefits contributions. At the time of this writing, it is unclear exactly how this might affect FSAs and other financial forms of employer-supported child care.

16. For a fuller explanation of FSAs and discrimination clauses, see Friedman (1985:27–32).

17. For accounts of how the changing nature of the work force has affected employee benefits in general, see Dallas L. Salisbury (ed.), *America in Transition: Implications for Employee Benfits* (Washington, DC: Employee Benefit Research Institute,1982).

18. Bruce Esterline, former executive director, Corporate Child Development Fund for Texas, testimony, in U.S. House of Representatives, Select Committee on Children, Youth, and Families, *Child Care: Exploring Private and Public Sector Approaches* (Washington, DC: U.S. Government Printing Office, 1984), 17–20.

19. Many people take exception to the labeling of pregnancy as a disability. While this label may exist to ensure nondiscrimination, it has the effect of casting a negative image on what is a personally and socially desirable experience for most women.

20. However, a recent United States Supreme Court Decision (Garland v. California Federal Savings) upheld as nondiscriminatory a California rule that requires employers to grant up to four months of unpaid leave to women "disabled" by pregnancy and childbirth, and to reinstate them in their particular jobs if at all possible. This decision may have implications for the treatment of maternity leave in other states in the future.

21. For a good discussion of the negative implications of part-time work for the status of women in general, see Vicki Smith, "The Circular Trap: Women and Part-time Work," *Berkeley Journal of Sociology* 28 (1983):1–17.

22. Anderson (1983), while she looks at both, does not present comparisons between employers who support child care and those who do not. Rather, she compares the level of involvement among different industry groups.

23. The sample of employers in the Delaware Valley survey was selected from all mid-size businesses (defined as having 100 to 1,000 employees) listed in the *Delaware Valley Business Firms Directory*, published by the Greater Philadelphia Chamber of Commerce (24th ed., 1985–1986). Businesses are listed in this directory by county and by division and major group—that is, type of industry—as defined by the

TABLE 3.6

Comparison of Division Distribution of Businesses in the Delaware Valley and in the Sample

Division	Delaware Valley	Sample
Construction / Contracting	5.8% (90)	1.0% (1)
Manufacturing	39.6% (617)	33.3% (33)
Transportation / Communication	4.9% (76)	7.1% (7)
Wholesale / Retail	14.9% (232)	12.1% (12)
Finance / Insurance / Real Estate	7.8% (121)	17.2% (17)
Service / Education / Medical	21.7% (338)	22.2% (22)
High Technology*	5.3% (83)	7.1% (7)
Total	100% (1,557)	100% (99)

*The high technology division is not defined separately from manufacturing in the *Business Firms Directory*, but the researcher felt there was a sufficiently significant difference between these two divisions—much of high technology work is nonmanufacturing—to treat them separately.

Standard Industrial Classification Manual. A representative sample of 200 companies was drawn from among these counties and divisions. In the survey call, 85 of the 200 companies elected not to participate in the study, and an additional 16 answered only one initial identifying question and then decided not to continue. Thus, the remaining 99 employers became the final, usable sample. As Table 3.6 shows, this sample closely approximated the actual proportion of all mid-size businesses and their distribution by division in the 11 county area. (For more details, see J. Auerbach 1987.)

24. See Barbara F. Reskin and Heidi Hartmann (eds.), *Women's Work, Men's Work: Sex Segregation on the Job* (Washington, DC: National Academy Press, 1986).

Chapter 4

The Motivations for and the Barriers to Employer-Supported Child Care

In Part I we investigated some of the social and historical changes leading to the emergence and proliferation of employer-supported child care in the 1980s. And in the chapter preceding this one we identified the characteristics and program types of sponsoring companies. But the significance of employer-supported child care—and its prospects in the future—cannot be understood without knowing *why* employers do or do not become involved. This chapter, therefore, examines the motivations for and the barriers to employer-supported child care as articulated by employers themselves.

As the following discussion makes clear, while employers cite different reasons for their involvement in child care, all allude to the rationale of enlightened self-interest. That is, the organizations that provide child care recognize that family life and work life are no longer separable, that tensions between them affect the work performance of employees, and that it may be in the organizations' best interest to do what they can to alleviate those tensions. Companies are coming to recognize that they derive economic benefit from paying attention to the needs of both their employees and the communities in which they operate. Thus, while the provision of child care may appear to be a progressive step by employers to help their employees, it is essentially a practical one.

When looking at the barriers to employer-supported child care, we see the same rationale operating. That is, like support of child care, resistance to it is based on issues of organizational self-interest. Whatever specific reasons employers give for their lack of involvement, they all imply that offering child care is not perceived to be necessary for the sustenance and stability of their company.

WHY EMPLOYERS DO SUPPORT CHILD CARE: THE MOTIVATIONS

In 1985 I conducted a series of in-depth interviews with 20 employers (in 18 states) who already provide some type of child care benefit to their employees. The purpose of these interviews was to determine the reasons behind employers' support and the processes of decision making involved.

The sample was nonrandomly selected from the list of employer-supported child care programs provided in Burud et al. (1984) and from companies mentioned in articles in the popular press (such as news and business magazines, and numerous local and national newspapers) between 1981 and 1985. Decision makers within the selected companies were interviewed over the telephone for about one hour. These decision makers represented the employers.

In order to determine the reasons for their involvement, employers were asked to describe the history of their program, that is, the events leading up to its implementation. Out of this account came information about the process of decision making as well. (See J. Auerbach 1986 for details of methodology.)

The following discussion of the motivations for employer-supported child care draws directly from 14 of my interviews (although it also takes into account information obtained from other available studies). Since individuals and their companies were promised anonymity, job titles and company pseudonyms are used. Profiles of these employers and their programs are shown in Tables 4.1 and 4.2, respectively. Most of the employers I interviewed offered a child care center either on the work site or near it. While this sample therefore may be of more "model" employers, I believe that the kinds of comments made by the interviewees about their reasons for getting involved in child care in the first place are typical of employers offering the whole range of programs. (Furthermore, to my knowledge, there are no other comparable interview data.)

Motivation to sponsor child care, as articulated by employers in my interviews and elsewhere, generally falls into the following categories: recruitment and retention of desirable personnel, reducing absenteeism and turnover among employees, a sense of social responsibility, and demands from existing personnel.

Recruitment and Retention

The primary reason employers give for supporting child care is recruitment and retention of desirable employees. Renee Magid (1983), for example, found that the greatest motivation expressed by the 204 employers responding to her survey was that child care "improved [their] position to attract talented employees." This was ranked first or second out of five reasons by more of the respondents than were other reasons. Indeed, child care can serve the interest of employers by enhancing recruitment efforts, particularly those devoted to tapping heavily female segments of the labor market such as nursing, clerical work, and high technology manufacturing. The situation of nursing illustrates this best.

In 1979 and 1980, this country experienced an acute shortage of nurses (Kalisch and Kalisch 1980).[1] Many hospitals and medical centers were struggling to figure out how best to recruit from a limited supply, and a number settled on offering child care as a competitive solution. Nurses who are parents are in particular need of good child care arrangements because many of them are single parents and many have unusual and irregular work shifts—including nights. The latter often precludes them from using available child care programs, which mostly are open only during regular business hours. A number of medical establishments therefore chose child care as a particularly attractive recruitment tool during this crisis.

Six of the nine employers I interviewed who gave recruitment and retention as their primary reason for supporting child care were medical establishments, either hospitals or nursing homes. Located in Mississippi, South Dakota, Kansas, Colorado, Nebraska, and Connecticut, each of these employers

TABLE 4.1
Employer Characteristics

Name	Region	Type of Company	Number of Employees	Women Employees	Average Age	Unionization
Community Hospital	Midwest	Service	2,050	89%	32	0
Computer Devices	Midwest	High Tech	55,858	n/a	n/a	n/a
Fabric Works	Midwest	Manufacturing	450	85%	n/a	n/a
Good Hope Hospital	Midwest	Service	1,676	83%	n/a	0
Island Fruit	West	Manufacturing	500	37%	50	50%
Midwest Manufacturing	Midwest	Manufacturing	87,000	n/a	n/a	n/a
New York Glass	East	Manufacturing	7,138	33%	n/a	39%
Northeast Catholic Hospital	East	Service	2,940	77%	n/a	0
Northwest County	West	Government	1,992	50%	42	84%
Plains State Hospital	Midwest	Service	2,947	82%	37	0
Software Sales	East	High Tech	700	56%	28	0
Southern Catholic Hospital	South	Service	1,176	83%	n/a	0
Southern Financial	South	Finance	5,200	67%	33	0
Southwest Engineering	South	Manufacturing	400	n/a	n/a	n/a

Note: n/a = not available

TABLE 4.2
Program Characteristics

Name	Program	Year Began	Reason for Program°	Number of Children	Age of Children	Cost to Parent per Child	Cost to Company
Community Hospital	Off-site Center	1980	RR	155	6 wks.-11 yrs.	$25 entrance; $1.35 per hour	40% of total costs
Computer Devices	Consortium Center	1971	AT	130	3 mos.-13 yrs.	n/a; Title XX families	start-up only
Fabric Works	On-site Center	1980	AT	106	2 yrs.-6 yrs.	$25 per week	$25 per week/ per child
Good Hope Hospital	On-site Center	1981	RR	475*	6 wks.-12 yrs.	n/a	n/a, building services
Island Fruit	On-site Center	1980	RR	36	2 yrs.-5 yrs.	$150 per mo.	60% of costs
Midwest Manufacturing	Info. & Referral	1982	ED	75 families per month	n/a	arranged with provider	n/a
New York Glass	Off-site Center	1980	RR	35	3 yrs.-5 yrs.	$142 per week	$17 per week/per child; in-kind; legal
Northeast Catholic Hospital	Off-site Center	1980	RR	30	3 yrs.-5 yrs.	$13 per day	43% of costs
Northwest County	Off-site Center	1981	ED	35	1 yr.-5 yrs.	$1206 - 405 per mo.	20% of costs ($6,000 per mo.)
Plains State Hospital	Off-site Center	1980	RR	99	18 mos.-6 yrs.	$10 per day	$600 per mo.
Software Sales	On-site Center	1981	ED	120	6 wks.-6 yrs.	$1 per day	n/a
Southern Catholic Hospital	On-site Center	1980	RR	105	6 wks.-5 yrs.	$42.50 per wk.	n/a - start-up only
Southern Financial	Off-site Center	1983	RR	41	15 mos.-5 yrs.	$45 per wk.	$55 per wk./ per child
Southwest Engineering	On-site Center	1973	SR	50	2 yrs.-5 yrs.	$55 per wk.	balance of costs; space

Note: ° = RR—recruitment and retention; AT—absenteeism and turnover;
ED—employee demand; SR—social responsibility.
* = Different shifts, usually 130 at a time.
n/a = not available.

mentioned the need to attract nurses, especially registered nurses (RNs), around 1980. In two cases, child care was an idea presented by administration or human resources management, irrespective of current employees' needs. In the others, current employees were simultaneously expressing need either by bringing up the subject to their supervisors or by answering employer-initiated child care needs assessment surveys. Although some demand may have been expressed previous to these inquiries, it was only once the needs of both employer and employee corresponded that support for child care was forthcoming.

The director at Southern Catholic Hospital in Mississippi made this process particularly clear:

We considered sponsoring child care when there was a critical nursing shortage in Mississippi. This was early 1980. Our motivation was to find something that would be unique to this hospital, so when nurses came into our city or were looking at the other hospitals in this area, there would be something that would stand out that would appeal to them. We also hoped this would help keep the nurses that we presently had, that it would provide motivation to stay.

In this case, the proposal for child care was initiated by the hospital administration; they had not been approached by nurses themselves. In fact, this employer had previously conducted a needs assessment survey among its employees and at that time did not get much response. Once this later initiative was taken, however, nurses were surveyed once again and this time there was much greater interest.

Community Hospital in South Dakota experienced a similar process. This employer is the largest community referral hospital in the state and must maintain a large staff (approximately 2,000) to be able to handle the number of special cases referred to it from other hospitals. Again, in 1980, this employer found it particularly difficult to get RNs. The vice-president of human resources explained:

We had been talking about the nursing shortage which had been extremely critical. We had been giving bonuses and doing all kinds of things, trying to get RNs to work here at Community Hospital because we were continuing to grow. We have some specific programs that are unique only to our hospital for the entire state, such as the dialysis, the neonatal, and the open heart surgery. In order to provide these kinds of services, we have to have the staff. So it was basically a question of need. We were doing everything in our power to get RNs, and child care was the one thing that we were short of.

The subject of child care kept surfacing at supervisory training sessions, and it became clear that a number of young mothers were having difficulty finding places for their children. The hospital proceeded to compile some demographic data and determined that the average age of its 89 percent female employees was under 30—the prime childbearing years. Thus child care seemed an attractive benefit to offer. Before drawing up a formal proposal to renovate two houses on the hospital's property for on-site child care, the Human Resources Department conducted a needs assessment survey. It found a definite need among the employees, especially for infant care. This need was incorporated into the hospital's subsequent child care policy, and the decision to provide on-site child care was ultimately made by executive management.

In two other cases—Northeast Catholic Hospital in Connecticut and Plains State Hospital in Kansas—the idea of offering child care as a recruitment and retention device was initially raised by the Human Resources Department. At Plains State Hospital, child care was only one of a number of ideas brainstormed at discussions about how best to attract RNs. At Northeast Catholic Hospital, child care was considered for recruitment and retention purposes at the urging of both Human Resources and a female physician. In both of these cases, after discussions were held between Human Resources personnel and other officials within the hospital administration, as well as with child care experts in the community, the proposal for child care was approved by the top levels of administration—the Administrative Council in one case, the director of the hospital in the other.

In only one medical establishment—Good Hope Hospital in Nebraska—was child care support initiated directly and independently by nurses. In this case it is doubtful that the request by employees alone would have been enough to get the hospital to sponsor child care. Rather, only after this request was seen in light of the immediate recruitment and retention needs of the hospital was it taken seriously. A hospital vice-president explained:

I would say that the history of how the child care came to be is related to the shortage of nursing and other professional staff here at our hospital and nationwide a few years ago. Our nurses, along with some other employees, had asked that we consider such a project. So [we] did a feasibility study and discovered that the need and the enthusiasm among employees was certainly there. Also, we were concerned with recruitment and retention. But initially, child care was suggested by employees. They went to the Director of Nursing Services who brought it to the attention of the Chief Executive Officer and the other Vice Presidents in executive conference. And finally, it went to the Board of Directors for approval.

Thus, the proposal for child care at this hospital had to be carried through many levels of approval after its initial suggestion by employees. Unless people at every stage recognized some benefit to the hospital or its employees, it is unlikely that the proposal would have received final approval.

Medical establishments are not the only employers to face recruitment and retention problems. All industries have a continuing need to find and keep the most desirable work force. While the definition of what constitutes a desirable employee differs among employers, depending upon their particular labor needs, in all cases it is the quality and stability of the work force that is ultimately the issue. For these contribute to productivity and, presumably, ultimately to profit. Thus, any employer wishing to stabilize a work force that it recognizes to be at risk for child care problems might see it as in its best interest to institute a child care program in an attempt to eliminate some of that risk.

Three such nonmedical employers I interviewed identified recruitment and retention as their primary motivation for instituting a child care program. In each case, the particular type of employee recruited was different, but all include those for whom child care might be a serious concern.

One of these employers is Southern Financial, a large banking and financial services institution in Georgia. One-third of its 5,200 employees work in a central city operations center, and a majority of its work force is female. According to the vice-president of human resources, the subject of sponsoring child care came up from time to time in conversations between the director of human resources and the chairman of the board of the bank. In 1982, child care was more formally discussed as only one of a number of issues brought up as part of a "comprehensive plan to enhance the quality of worklife" and to recruit and retain "very qualified people." The latter was considered of particular importance, given the nature of the banking industry as growth oriented, labor intensive, and plagued by high rates of employee turnover and absenteeism. The vice-president of human resources explained why child care was considered at her company:

The Director of Human Resources and the Chairman of the Board were looking at ways in which we could enhance the quality of worklife; in other words, make this company a place where people want to come to work and want to stay employed. Child care was mentioned as only one of a number of issues. It was brought up by the Chairman. Our industry is 67 percent female. Our average age is 33. So, we're a very young, female-oriented company. Plus we acknowledge the fact that women are permanently in the workforce.

After considering other options, the company decided to sponsor an on-site center. For this employer, then, a child care benefit was something that could clearly assist in the recruitment of the type of employee it deemed desirable—young women. Moreover, an on-site child care center might help to retain those employees by alleviating one of the problems that contribute to their high rates of absenteesim and turnover—having unreliable child care arrangements that may require them to miss work if they fall through. As the vice-president of human resources saw it:

It adds peace of mind to know their child is really within walking distance of them; that they can go and have lunch with their children any day that they want to; that we have an open door policy; they can visit any time that they want; that if the child for some reason isn't feeling well, all they have to do is just run over to the center and check up on them. They don't have to take the entire day to go a long distance to another place to check on the child.

At the same time, this employer realized the limitations of child care—or any employee benefit, for that matter—in solving all retention problems in what may simply be a bad work situation:

It's certainly not going to make up for a bad job; it's not going to be a panacea. It's not going to make a happy employee out of someone who is miserable. But it could make it easier for the employee to balance work and family life during that part of life.

Another employer that chose to sponsor a child care program for recruitment purposes did so to attract managerial and professional level women. In the early 1980's, New York Glass, a large manufacturing company in New York state, found that potential recruits and existing employees were consistently mentioning that finding child care in the area of the company was a real problem. While the Personnel Department had been investigating the possibility of company-supported child care, the real impetus, according to a company official, came from the chairman of the board, who had become aware of the problem after a number of informal conversations with concerned people in the community. (The company is located in a small community in which people socialize a great deal.) The human resources manager for the "Technology Group" stated that this was typical procedure for her company—many policies and programs are generated by employee concern, with subsequent involvement by the chairman once he recognizes that the issue is of concern to the community as well.

The human resources manager, who was responsible for recruiting more female employees to the company, was assigned responsibility for researching the child care issue. Once she established that there was a real shortage of child care in the community, and had investigated different employer—supported child care options, she recommended that her company sponsor a child care center. The recommendation went to the company's foundation, whose board is made up of the chairman and several senior managers in the company. The board decided to sponsor an off-site center at an existing church in the middle of town (within one-half to three miles of all except two of the company's facilities). Since the program had foundation support, it was required to open with and maintain a 50/50 ratio of company and community children.

The third industrial employer for whom recruitment and retention was the primary reason for supporting a child care center was Island Fruit Company, a large food production company in Hawaii. In this case, the recruitment need was not for women workers specifically, but for young workers of both sexes. The company had an older work force at this site, many of whom were beginning to retire in the early 1980s. In attempting to recruit younger workers, Island Fruit found itself in stiff competition with surrounding resort areas. The benefits administrator was in charge of identifying and developing programs that might attract the younger workers, and he initially focused on fitness programs. His research took him to a Texas aerobics center. While there, he was sent to observe the fitness program of a nearby engineering company and, as he told it:

It was okay. But what really struck me was their pre-school facility. It was an on-site center. So when I came back and spoke to the President about fitness programs, I also spoke in detail about the on-site child care center I had seen. It hit perfectly with him. He thought it was the greatest thing he'd heard, because we're going through a lot of retirements and we need such an attraction as child care in order to compete for those employees who work for the resort areas and for the retail industry.

This was an instance in which the company had not explicitly set out to examine child care support but, once exposed to a successful example, came to realize its potential for attracting young employees. The company president made the decision to sponsor an on-site center, but this followed a community needs assessment and a demographic evaluation of company employees to determine the need for child care. In examining what existed in the community, the benefits administrator found that all centers had waiting lists. So, rather than opting for a voucher or vendor program, the company felt it had to supply more spaces by starting a center. Additionally, the company had some particular needs with regard to its hours of employment that made the use of existing facilities difficult or impossible for its employees. Consequently, the benefits administrator explained:

> We decided to build a facility and develop it on-site, because we felt it would give us control over the quality, which was very important to us. Also, we could control the hours. And in addition, by opening a facility for our employees, we were opening up spaces within the community that they may have taken.

Island Fruit Company has the unusual background of having provided on-site child care at different locations as early as before World War II, although the person I interviewed knew nothing of the details of the earlier centers or what happened to them. Company involvement as he knew it became significant only beginning in 1970, when it leased a building and three-quarters of an acre of property in one location to a Baptist church to run a preschool for company employees. Additionally, in 1979, the company began developing a new resort area on one of the islands and opened a child care center there for the resort workers. The program we discussed in detail was the latest one, established at a main production location in 1981.

All of these employers who mentioned recruitment and retention as their primary motivation for instituting a child care program needed to have something clearly unique in their area or industry with which to attract and keep desirable employees. All of them, except one, were competing specifically for young, female employees, for whom child care was or might have become a prime concern, given the shortage of programs available. What is especially interesting, however, is that all of these employers suported on- or off-site centers, as contrasted with another child care option. Many considered and researched other programs, but all decided to provide centers either because they had existing space that could be easily be renovated or because they felt that they had to increase the number of child care spaces available in their community in order to recruit successfully.

All employers with whom I spoke had mostly positive remarks about the success of their child care centers in recruiting new employees. However, at the time, none of them had conducted formal research to determine the extent to which the existence of their child care center was directly responsible for the recruitment of particular employees; consequently, all of their evaluative comments were primarily intuitive or anecdotal.

One such comment came from the human resources manager at New York Glass:

It ends up being a very effective recruiting tool, because it says, "we expect you're going to come back to work for us" to the professional woman. If nothing else, a new-hire coming in who isn't married and doesn't know yet if she wants to have kids can say, "at least the company is interested in that; it must want me to come back to work." So it is a recruiting tool for us. Why, $30,000 [the initial contribution to the center] is a drop in the bucket compared with what you pay to recruit. You can justify it just on that.

Other evaluations of the effectiveness of the child care centers were made with regard to retention, as in this comment from the director at Southern Catholic Hospital in Mississippi:

A lot of times, it keeps people here who ordinarily would leave, because their children are in a situation where they're happy. And sometimes a mother will stay in a work situation that she's not as pleased with just for the child's welfare.

This is indeed a candid remark, because it does not speak of the child care program as having directly improved the work situation or morale of the employee but, rather, as having provided a stable care situation for the child—one that a parent does not want to disrupt. As far as the employer is concerned, the important thing is that the employee is still there. This, of course, hints at a pernicious implication of employer-supported child care, that it might be used as a method of retaining and molifying dissatisfied workers who, if not for their concern about disrupting their children's stable child care arrangements, would leave. (So far, there is very little anecdotal information, such as the director's comment above, to suggest that employers are thinking along these lines, but many observers of employer-supported child care are concerned about the possibility none-theless.)

Perhaps the lack of hard data on the recruitment success of these companies' child care programs signifies the extent to which they rely on their own perception of success. In other words, if they perceive that their needs have been fulfilled, that is, that they have effectively recruited and retained the staff they re-quire, they can assume their projects are working without hav-ing to formally study them. As one employer put it: "Well, there's no question that the company officers all have seen the results. We've had an adequate staff." Before they instituted the child care program, they faced a shortage of nurses; after they insti-tuted it, they did not.

This is not to say that no companies have formally studied the results of their child care programs. On the contrary, some have attempted to measure the recruitment effects of child care in actual dollars. The 1981-1982 NESCCP study received the following information from human resource departments in 415 companies they studied: 85 percent reported that child care had a positive effect on recruitment; 32 percent considered child care more effective than three-fourths of the other recruitment incentives they used; 73 percent considered child care more effective than half of the other recruitment incentives they used; and 10 employers estimated an annual savings of $16,400 per company in recruitment costs from having a child care benefit (Burud et al. 1984:23).

The project selected four companies as case studies. All had well established child care programs and kept data on them. For the three cases in which the effect of child care on recruit-ment was available, they found that in one case, 95 percent of job seekers applied to work at the company because of the child care program; in another, 20 percent of the previous recruitment effort was needed after the child care program was established; and in the third, the estimated annual savings in recruitment due to child care was $30,000 (Burud et al. 1984:23).

In a subsequent study in 1984, NESCCP surveyed 691 employees with children in employer-supported programs. Thirty-eight percent said child care was a factor in continuing to work at their company, 63 percent said they had a more positive attitude toward their company because of its support for child care, and over 50 percent said they recommended their employer to others because of its child care support (Bureau of National Affairs 1984:6–7).

Thus, there are some data that support employers' impressions of the usefulness of sponsoring child care for the recruitment and retention of employees.

Absenteeism and Turnover

Once they are recruited, stability is a common problem for female employees who have young children. A few companies have instituted child care programs to alleviate problems of absenteeism, tardiness, and turnover among this population, since these are seen to contribute to reduced productivity (and ultimately profits). Again, while some employers say they have instituted child care for this reason, few have kept data on its effect. However, for those who have, the results are telling.[2]

The NESCCP found in its 1981–1982 study that among the employers it studied, 53 percent reported that child care had a positive effect on absenteeism, 18 percent considered child care more effective than three-fourths of the other absentee control methods they used, and 56 percent considered child care more effective than half of the other absentee control methods they used (Burud et al. 1984:26).

In one well publicized case, Intermedics (a heart pacemaker manufacturer in Freeport, Texas) introduced an on-site child care center in 1979 to combat tardiness, absenteeism, and turnover among its predominantly female (70 percent) and single-parent employees. In the first year of the center's operation, Intermedics experienced a 23 percent decrease in employee turnover and 15,000 fewer work-hours of absenteeism from the previous year. In the second year, the turnover rate decreased 37 percent. By 1984, the turnover rate for parents using the center was one-sixth the rate of the remaining work force. Altogether,the company estimated it had saved over $2 million in reduced turnover since the child care center opened (Burud et al. 1984:39–40).

Two employers I interviewed gave absenteeism and turnover as their primary reason for instituting a child care program. After the first year of operation of its child care center, Computer Devices collected specific data to measure its direct effect on parent absenteeism and turnover. A research team from a nearby university was hired to compile the data. To measure absenteeism, they computed hours absent/hours scheduled for each parent before and after enrollment of children at the center. In 1972 the difference in absenteeism represented a 21.4 percent reduction from preenrollment rates. In 1973 monthly absenteeism rates were computed and compared for parents using the center and parents not using the center. The average monthly rate for center users was 4.4 percent, and for nonusers it was 6.0 percent.

To assess any differences in turnover rates caused by use of the child care center, monthly turnover rates of a sample of mothers using the center were compared with those of women doing the same job but not using the center. The results for the 24-month period between January 1972 and December 1973 were significant: the monthly turnover rates for mothers using the center averaged 1.7 percent, substantially lower than the 5.4 percent average rate for other women.

In 1977, the second employer, Fabric Works, recognized that problems with turnover and absenteeism were resulting in damage to equipment in the plant. A large number of the employees were single-parent women at the low end of the wage scale. A management team interviewed employees and found that child care and transportation were two major problems contributing to their instability. The executive vice-president— a member of this team—investigated companies with child care centers that had experienced reductions in turnover and absenteeism. Once impressed by their success, he intended to set up the first industry-sponsored, on-site, 24-hour child care center, but felt he ran into too many regulatory barriers. Instead, he established a daytime-only, on-site center in 1980.

While data on the effect of the center on absenteeism and turnover were not available, the program was perceived to be a success. The executive vice-president saw the question of employee stability and productivity as related to morale in general. Thus, the institution and success of the child care program were viewed in the context of the company's overall philosophy and management:

Even the people who did not have children in the center treated us as more of a family, more of a team. And this is something we've tried to project all along—our employees are members of a team. It all just seems to mesh together with the child care center, because, if your kid is there with you at work, you become more involved with the welfare of the company you're working for.

Another way to view this, of course, is that if child care arrangements exist at the work site, one major source of distraction from work is alleviated, and parents can work more consistently, whether or not it is because they are truly involved with the welfare of the company.

The benefits of reduced absenteeism and turnover rates were not experienced only by employers who elected to support child care explicitly for that purpose. Community Hospital instituted its child care center in 1980 primarily as a recruitment device. However, this employer systematically studied the effects of its program on absenteeism and turnover as well. The data show a companywide 7.8 percent annual decrease in turnover since the center was opened. In 1982, parents using the child care center had a turnover rate of 24 percent, compared with an average 33 percent for the other employees in the company. Before the child care center opened, parents eligible to use it had a 40 percent turnover rate. Since then, the employer estimated the company had saved $159,600 annually through reduced turnover of parents using the center.

Similarly, absenteeism rates declined, also benefiting the hospital financially. Management estimated the absenteeism rates of parents using the center decreased from 6 percent to 1 percent, while the rate for other employees remained at 4 percent throughout. Additionally, the value of reduced absenteeism among parents using the center was estimated to be nearly $90,000 annually.

A probable explanation for the high rate of absenteeism among female employees in these companies and others is that their children are often ill. Even if other child care arrangements are made, in the event of an illness, a mother will most often leave work or stay home to attend to her sick child. Many studies have shown that infants and young children are ill six to nine times a year, and that their illnesses can cause a serious loss of wages for mothers. For example, a study conducted by the Learning Tree Day Care Centers in the Minneapolis area found that 422 parents with a total of 592 children (age 6 weeks to 13 years) reported that their children were ill for 3,030 days in the previous year, or 5 days per year per child. These parents, 83 percent of whom were women, used 2,447 of their sick days to care for their children, with a loss of wages for 983 of those days (Parents in the Workplace 1983:6).

Besides directly affecting the mother's wages, absenteeism due to children's illnesses has contributed to the notion that women do not represent a reliable labor pool. This image benefits neither the mother, who desires occupational mobility, nor her employer, which desires a stable and productive work force. The fact that a mother must leave work to attend to her sick child indicates the shortage of available alternatives. While there are a few exceptions, sick care is one area of child care that has received very little attention from employers.

The 1981–1982 NESCCP study found only 5 out of 415 employers currently supporting child care programs for sick children. One supported a community program, and the other four provided care in their child care centers. Other employers contributed financially to existing community programs that provide home health service, or they had temporary holding rooms at their centers where sick children could be isolated and cared for until the parents could pick them up (Burud et al. 1984).

Similarly, only 3 of the 20 employers in my sample provided some type of sick child care. Christian Nursing Home in Idaho had immediate medical care available as well as a separate place with a bed and a nurse at its on-site center. Greenland Hospital in Colorado had an arrangement for care in its emergency wing. Midwest Manufacturing in Minnesota had a pilot program that placed a health care worker in the sick child's home. Of the $6.25 per hour, the company paid $4.25 and the parent paid the remaining $2.00.

Besides providing sick care in their own day care facilities or subsidizing at-home care by professionals, employers can consider other options. The most flexible one, and one for which there is a great deal of advocacy, is structuring personnel policies to facilitate parent care for a sick child in its own home. Some examples of such policies already in existence include allowing an employee to use sick time for reasons of illness in his or her immediate family, not just for himself or herself, granting employees an allotment of paid "occasional absences" to be monitored by supervisors, and combining allowable paid sick days, special absences, and holidays into a single category of "personal days" to be used at the discretion of the employee (Parents in the Workplace 1983).

Although the incidence of sick children has a direct effect on absenteeism rates, employers are wary of involving themselves in sick child care for a number of reasons. These include the increasing costs of employee benefits in general, concern about ensuring equity in employee absence policies, and fear of turning what the company considers a benefit into something employees will consider a right (Parents in the Workplace 1983). Additionally, there are the practical concerns of sick care being a fluctuating demand (the need for sick child care is not regular or predictable) and liability issues, especially for on-site care (Burud et al. 1984).

But even with these concerns, employers are increasingly aware of the direct costs to them of employee absenteeism due to child care problems. Many have seen those costs reduced by instituting a company-sponsored child care program, although, overall, the problem of sick child care remains unresolved.

Social Responsibility

In addition to the desire to maintain a good, stable work force, employers sometimes mention "social responsibility" as a motivation to support child care. What they mean by this term varies. There is no single definition of social responsibility, although among those offered by academicians and business people there are common themes. In their broadest sense, these definitions suggest that social responsibility refers to a business's sense of obligation to its employees and to the community in which it operates. This involves being able to adapt to, and even to anticipate, the changing needs and expectations of both (Rivlin 1983). This is how employers themselves interpret social responsibility in the context of their support for child care. Three employers I interviewed gave a version of social responsibility as their main reason for supporting a child care program.

At Southwest Engineering, a medium size (400 employees) manufacturer of electrical utility burners located in Texas, the idea of sponsoring a child care center originated with the president of the company in the early 1970s. He had traveled to other countries and was particularly impressed with the manner in which China had accommodated working women by instituting collectivized child care at work sites or in neighborhoods. According to the center director, this visit caused the president to think about the needs of his own employees.

He wanted to try to help his employees as much as he could with whatever problems they had. He realized that child care was one of them. Ours is a small company. It's kind of a personal company, where the President always kept up with what was going on and with what the needs of his employees were. Also, he listened to supervisors talking about the problems of parenthood his workers had expressed to them.

As the director noted, because this employer was the president, he carried some weight. So once he developed a proposal—which was part of a larger plan for employee services, including a fitness program—there was little trouble getting final approval from the board of directors. The activism of the president was not, however, confined to proposing the child care center. In fact, he designed the program himself after a few years of research and contemplation. At this time, employer-supported child care was a relatively new idea, particularly in the South, and there were virtually no models for the president to follow. Thus, Southwest Engineering's eventual involvement in child care can be attributed to the leadership and dedication of a particular individual in a position of power to institutionalize his progressive ideas.

For the director, even the manner in which the company went about designing the program reflected the progressive attitude of the president toward his employees. A parent group was formed of people from all departments—males and females, and a representative mix of ethnic groups in the company. Representatives of this parent group went out to the community and looked at the available supply of child care so they could help formulate what they would want in their own center. They also brought in speakers and child care experts so they could learn about various program options and philosophies. The group worked together for about two years developing their plan and disbanded only when the company's child care center opened on-site in 1973.

Originally, the center was for employees' children only; but after a year and a half, the company decided to open it to the community as well (although it planned always to retain about 75 percent of the spaces for employees). The director felt that this was a good move on the part of Southwest Engineering: She believed that opening up the center made the community more receptive to the company, so that "it seems we're part of everybody else; we're not exclusive."

What is particularly interesting about this company is that even after the president left and subsequent administrators took over, and even when the company experienced many layoffs and a downturn in business, for years the child care program was retained. According to the director, it was not even threatened. This seems to have been because the new administrators—none of whom were the original commitment makers on the center—felt that the center had been a very effective recruitment and publicity tool. In fact, the director claimed, "Some new employees said they came to the company because of child care, not because of the company itself." And, she said, once there, many of these employees stayed because their children were in the center:

Even when there is some problem with their job, they won't leave it because they don't want to put their children in a different place; they are pleased with where they are. I think at the times when morale has been at the lowest, the thing that probably has kept us going is the fact that the child care center is a benefit that's being offered to them.

Thus, while this company-supported child care program was initiated by a particular official with a personal concern for his employees, it was maintained even after his departure for other, company-oriented reasons—recruitment, retention, and public relations. However, since the time of the interview, the center has closed, to the great dismay of many employees who chose to join Southwest Engineering because of its child care benefit. According to company officials, the closure finally became necessary after prolonged financial difficulties made even its beneficial aspects less compelling than its cost.

Public Relations

One thing that became clear from interviews with Southwest Engineering and other employers who cited social responsibility as their motivation to support child care is that something more than altruism was operating. For communities and employees have many needs, and the choice to address one over another is not made without regard to its relative benefit to the company. In this case, the support of child care offers the benefit of good public relations. And, as we all know, good public relations—like improved employee morale and productivity—is believed ultimately to translate into profits.

However, while good public relations is a perceived benefit, it is almost never the primary motivation for an employer to support child care. None of the employers I interviewed gave public relations as the primary reason for their involvement, although many did mention it as a by-product. This is similar to Magid's (1983) findings. Certainly, in the context of recruitment especially, a favorable company image is important; but it is recruitment of personnel, not public relations in the abstract, that is the goal (and thus the primary motivation to support child care).

Nevertheless, articles and pamphlets encouraging employers to consider developing child care programs make much of the public relations benefits, as do publications put out by companies already sponsoring child care. For example, one publication by a child care advocate claims:

The provision of child care can change the morale of employees through reduced child care worries and increased respect for the employer. It can humanize the workplace, help the company develop good public relations, provide a competitive edge in recruiting employees, and place the company in a favorable Equal Employment Opportunity position. (Friedman 1981:4)

Whether or not providing child care actually does all these things, it does result in great publicity. Employer-supported child care programs are the subject of many articles in such widely circulated publications as *Newsweek, Time, Inc., Working Woman,* and *The Wall Street Journal.*

Employee Demand

Unfortunately, there is very little research or data that make clear the extent to which employee demand is responsible for the initiation of a company's child care program. Most of the discussion so far has suggested that programs are initiated from above. That is, somehow employers come to identify child care problems as a barrier to the full productivity and stability of their work force, and they institute programs on their own initiative to remedy the situation. Even where child care concern is expressed by employees to their superiors, it is not presented as a *demand* that the employer do something about it.

In fact, the notion of demand is misleading, for in the absence of an institutionalized mechanism for making demands—such as a union—employees can at best recommend or suggest. A discussion of the role of unions as representatives of employees in their demand for child care is in the Appendix. For now, it is worth noting that their role has been very limited. I believe this is due to three factors: (1) the limited availability of collective bargaining funds; (2) the lack of unionization of many traditionally female occupations; and (3) the underrepresentation of women and "women's issues"—as child care is seen to be— in existing unions and on their agendas.

So, without a formal mechanism, employee demand is experienced by employers in a diluted form. On the list of motivations for employer-supported child care in Magid's (1983) survey, for example, the closest response to "employee demand" is "encouragement from employees" or "recommendation of employee task force." These responses ranked fifth and sixth, respectively, out of 14.

Similarly, in my study, five employers mentioned a diluted version of employee demand as their primary motivation to support child care. In fact, a more appropriate term for what they describe is employee *initiative*. In two companies, employees informally and formally expressed concern over child care problems, and in the other three, high-level employees who were experiencing child care problems took the initiative in developing a company-supported program.

In one company, formal channels existed through which employees' needs for child care were expressed. Midwest Manufacturing is a very large Minnesota-based company with over 87,000 employees. According to the child care coordinator, in the early 1980s employees' needs for child care became increasingly clear through a number of channels. The most formal was the Advisory Committee on Women's Concerns, a committee within the corporate structure that develops policies and programs related to the status of women and the affirmative action goals of the company. Child care came up in this context. Second, child care was mentioned by employees in the company's Employee Assistance Program, which attempts to deal with parents' problems that might affect their job performance. Finally, the company's confidential letter-writing program found a great increase in the number of letters requesting company involvement in child care.

From these expressions of interest, a temporary task force was assigned to look at child care. It recommended that Midwest Manufacturing hire a person to focus on child care needs within the company and begin with an information and referral service. This recommendation was based on the identification of a wide diversity of child care needs among employees.

Eventually, Midwest Manufacturing conducted a needs assessment survey in which the greatest demand was found to be for infant and small child care. At that point, the company decided to make a financial contribution to community members already providing care, and encouraged them to expand. Specifically, the company contributed to a local center to help it begin an infant care program. In 1985, 30 percent of the center's clientele were the children of Midwest Manufacturing employees. The success of this center suggested to the coordinator "that we can provide more services by dealing with the community and stimulating there rather than trying to duplicate services ourselves."

For three other employers who said employee initiative, if not demand, was their primary motivation for supporting child care, the existence of a high-level employee with a personal need for child care was crucial.

In one case, Northwest County—the only government sponsor I interviewed—instituted its child care program in 1981 at the behest of a county commissioner who was a single parent with two children, one preschool age at the time. According to his staff assistant, the commissioner had been concerned about child care for some time, and had earlier surveyed county employees about their needs. Once that was established, he researched various options and eventually presented a "budget modification" to the Board of County Commissioners to authorize a financial contribution to begin a child care center. The board passed the measure and gave the center $5,000 for seed money. The center was established on noncounty property as a cooperative, nonprofit agency for county employees and community members (county employees receive a discount).

Thus, in this case, one particular person in a position of power within his organization started the idea of supporting child care, researched it out of his office, searched for the location of the center, and lobbied effectively for the finances to establish it. Furthermore, he placed his child in the program, where, as his staff assistant said, "he participates as a parent rather than a politician."

A similar course of events occurred at Software Sales, a high technology company in North Carolina with 700 employees. As the headmistress of the preschool described it, the child care program was "employee-owner initiated." In early 1981, the company was privately owned by three people, one of whom had a young child. Her child care arrangement at the time was using a baby-sitter nearby and going back and forth to nurse her child. When she was about to have a second child, she and other young mothers in the company (which at the time had only 50 employees) decided to start a nursery on-site. As the thought of child care evolved, other mothers felt it would be desirable to have toddlers there. So, in the end, the company opted for an on-site all-day Montessori program, with separate facilities for infants/toddlers and preschool children.

According to the headmistress, the decision to provide child care at Software Sales was made by the owner. At the time, there was no formal process of decision making; the owners made all the decisions. Again, like Northwest County, the presence of a particular individual with a need for child care and the power to act on it explains the involvement of this company.

It is worth noting that in all of these cases, although the child care program was started to address the immediate needs of employees, other benefits of reduced absenteeism and turnover were also recognized.

WHY EMPLOYERS DON'T SUPPORT CHILD CARE: THE BARRIERS

At the same time there are reasons for employers to get involved in child care, there are significant barriers against it. This is evident in the fact that, while the number of employers providing child care continues to increase, it is still only a small proportion of all companies in the United States (an estimated 1 percent), even among those we would think most likely to get involved, based on the profile drawn in Chapter 3.

In order to have a better understanding of employers' role

in child care, it is therefore important to look at why companies do not get involved—according to employers themselves—as well as why they do. The following discussion of barriers to employer-supported child care comes mostly from two main sources. One source is the Delaware Valley survey (described in Chapter 3), in which randomly selected employers who do not have a child care program were asked to identify what they thought were significant barriers to employer-supported child care. The other source is in-depth interviews I conducted in 1985 with five employers who had considered initiating a child care benefit but ultimately decided not to. (See J. Auerbach 1986 for details of methodology.) These interviews with employers who actively considered child care can tell us about the real barriers that exist after an initial, favorable interest.

In these two sources, the most significant barriers mentioned by employers who do not support a child care program were cost, liability, lack of space, licensing and regulations, equity, perceived lack of demand, and lack of knowledge of options. Table 4.3 shows the number of employers in the Delaware Valley Survey who mentioned each of these barriers.

Cost

Cost is commonly mentioned because, rather than considering all options, most companies that consider child care approach their investigation with the idea that ultimately they will have an on-site center (Friedman 1983a), and once they realize the cost involved (which can easily run over $1 million for new construction and start-up expenses), many decide it is much too expensive. This is of course a particular problem for companies that experience periodic financial difficulties or fluctuations, as in the high technology sector.

Upstart Computer in California—one of the employers I interviewed—investigated child care involvement in 1984 after demand was increasingly expressed in informal ways by employees, primarily women. The manager of employee benefits and relocation explained: "It just seemed to be something people were talking about more and more. If you would go to a

TABLE 4.3
Barriers to Employer-Supported Child Care: Responses from the
Delaware Valley Survey

Barrier	Number of Employers Mentioning*
Cost	41
Liability	37
Space	36
Licensing and Regulation	32
Equity	39
Lack of Demand	46
Lack of Knowledge of Options	15

*These are the 69 employers who were neither offering nor considering a
  child care benefit. Each gave more than one response.

meeting that was to discuss benefits, child care would seem to
always come up."

   She took on the responsibility of researching possible options, although it was assumed that the company was ultimately
considering an on-site center. A needs assessment survey among
employees revealed a wide range of child care needs. The manager suggested to the vice-president of human resources that
the company come up with a plan reflecting that range, beginning perhaps with a spending account or referral service. The
company did consider this and other possibilities, but ultimately decided to table the child care issue because of major
structural and financial problems it was experiencing. At that
point, any child care option—especially an on-site center—
seemed extraordinary, since the company was losing $40 mil-
lion in its restructuring attempt. But rather than rejecting the

child care recommendation out of hand, essentially nothing was done on it. The manager of employee benefits and relocation felt: "It was not a conscious decision that we aren't considering child care because of this or that particular reason. It was just clear that nothing was going to be done on it because of what was going on in the company."

The tabling of the child care issue at that point was just that. A follow-up in 1986 revealed that Upstart Computers—now more financially stable—was not only reconsidering child care involvement, but in fact was planning to build an on-site center.

Another employer for whom cost was an issue in considering child care was Hi-Tech Chemical, also in California. Interest in child care was generated in 1984 by employees—again, mostly women, but with some upper management male support. A group of eight women drafted a formal proposal to the employee relations manager to study employee need. After conducting a needs assessment survey, they found that a variety of needs existed, and considered recommending that the company adopt a voucher option. Yet, they never got that far. As one of these eight women, a quality engineer, tells it, she met with the employee relations manager, who told her frankly that there was no way the company would consider any type of child care and that she and her colleagues were "wasting their time."

The quality engineer thought that this manager discouraged the employees because of cost considerations, since the company had cut many programs and had imposed an austerity program during that year. But she also felt that the committee might have been more successful if it had been able to push its recommendation to a higher level, where division managers had already informally expressed some support. As it was, this was impossible. The quality engineer, disappointed that the employee relations manager was so discouraging, felt that she could not push the issue because this manager was her supervisor. As a result, the child care proposal died, unable to be moved from one level in the organization to the next.

This experience again points to the importance of having support from people at higher levels of the company who are willing to push for consideration of child care. Without it, child care proposals can easily die.

Liability, Space, and Licensing

As with cost concerns, some of the other barriers to child care commonly mentioned by employers imply that they assume involvement means building or sponsoring a child care center as opposed to other options. Indeed, concern about liability—in terms of both the cost of insurance and the responsibility for children's well-being—is really applicable only to a center.[3] This is true also of concern about lack of space.

To some extent, it is also true of antipathy toward the bureaucratic hassle of state licensing and regulation. That is, supporting an on- or near-site child care center means having to deal directly with legal procedures that are often cumbersome and constricting. It is also the case that supporting a family day care network or an information and referral service involves issues of licensing and regulations. For example, should the employer include only licensed providers in its program, and should it monitor these providers itself?

But, when employers mention cost, liability, lack of space, and licensing as barriers to involvement, it is probably because they assume that the only employer-supported child care option is a center.

Equity

Another reason commonly mentioned by employers who do not have a child care program is the problem of equity. In some cases, the company is a multi-site operation, that is, it has different locations with different employee populations and child care needs. This raises questions about how it can practically and equitably offer a program to all employees.

This was an issue for two companies I studied. Commercial Credit, located in Maryland, determined that need for child care existed among its employees, but could not figure out a reasonable way to accommodate the diversity of that need existing in the 90 percent of its offices located in shopping malls all over the country. A similar problem existed with Statewide Insurance of New York, whose multiple locations had very different size employee populations.

While there are options for these employers—IBM in the same situations has created a national information and referral service for all of its employees—the multi-site problem is one many employers feel poses a major barrier to their involvement because of the cost and equity issues it raises.

But, more than arising from the multi-site issue, the problem of equity arises from the concern among companies and employees that their organization not provide a service that favors some people and not others. Child care serves only a small portion of a total work force at any one time.

Interestingly, most companies that do have a child care program have not seen the issue of equity come up (Friedman 1983a); in fact, it can be avoided if an employer chooses a flexible benefit program. Nevertheless, because many employers start out envisioning a child care center as their ultimate choice, the question of discriminatory benefits may arise.

This is what happened at World Credit in California. The subject of child care came up in 1983 at an all-company meeting in which an employee asked the president if it could be considered. The president agreed, and the head of personnel took on the responsibility of researching and making a recommendation. She, in turn, with the assistance of employee volunteers, studied different child care options, conducted a needs assessment survey, and observed existing child care centers in their community. In the course of this, she discovered that many of the employees who expressed child care need thought that the company was going to provide an on-site center free of charge. The company was in fact considering a voucher system or a less expensive on-site center in which parents would pay some of the charge. But in any case, once nonparent employees realized that the company was considering any type of child care, according to the head of personnel:

[It] resulted in a horrendous backlash from the non-parents who said, "It was the parent's choice to have a child. I have made a conscious choice not to. I'm taking care of my aging parents. I can't afford to have children. Now if you're going to pay for child care then why don't you pay for care for my parents? If you're going to give equal benefits, then make it equal. If you're giving something extra to the parents, then give us some extra fringe."

These sentiments were expressed both informally in conversations and formally in letters to the head of personnel. They were also expressed at plenary meetings that the president attended. Eventually, parents on the child care committee decided that the complaints of the nonparents were justified and withdrew their recommendations for company involvement.

While this case is a rare one, it does suggest that employers considering child care will have to be prepared to offer a similar benefit to nonparent employees. This will be a greater concern, I suspect, in newer companies with large proportions of young professional and managerial employees who may have chosen to be childless while pursuing a career. (Indeed, World Credit had primarily professional and managerial employees— 50 percent male and 50 percent female—whose average age was 35.)

Lack of Demand

Probably the most significant barrier to employer-supported child care is the perceived lack of demand from employees. Many employers who have not even considered providing a child care benefit indicate on surveys that they do not know what the child care needs of their emloyees are (Policy/Action Institute 1986). As can be seen in Table 4.3, of the 69 employers in the Delaware Valley survey who were neither offering nor investigating child care, 46 (67 percent) mentioned "lack of demand" as a barrier to their involvement. This was the most common barrier mentioned.

Employers assume that there is no child care problem among their employees unless it is brought to their attention. This is a particularly significant barrier, because it illustrates the extent to which employees are hesitant to bring up conflicts between work and family life, even if these directly affect their work performance. Female employees in professional and managerial positions have had to work very long and hard to get where they are in a company, and many feel they could only do this by not drawing attention to their family needs. These women— the ones who appear to be in positions of relative influence, if not power—are particularly hesitant to initiate any kind of demand for child care support from their employers (Hertz 1986).

At the same time, as mentioned earlier, lower level employees in most cases lack a formal mechanism such as a union for making such demands; and they fear negative sanctions that might come from taking any initiative (Anderson 1983). They, too, therefore refrain from making their need for child care assistance known to their employer. As one expert put it during testimony before the House of Representatives Select Committee on Children, Youth and Families in 1984:

For families that don't have satisfactory child care arrangements, it is hard for them to admit that, and this seems to work at all levels in companies, but the lower paid employees are really afraid to mention any kind of personal problems. You don't bring those problems to work because you can be replaced by somebody who doesn't have those problems.[4]

Men have been just as reluctant as women to press employers to consider providing a child care benefit. Although there is a cohort of young, progressive fathers present in the work force, there is no evidence that they are activists for child care. In most men's minds, child care is still a woman's responsibility, not theirs or their employers'. (Of course there are a few exceptions. Some of the employer-supported child care programs I studied were initiated by men, which is important but rare.)

Indeed, in John P. Fernandez's (1986) survey of 5,000 employees in five major corporations, men in management were the least likely of all categories of gender and occupational level to believe that their corporation has an obligation to play an active role in assisting employees in their child care needs. If these are the men who affect corporate policies, then we can see why little has been done in the way of child care support by most of the organizations that employ them.

The reasons both male and female employees do not demand child care as a benefit are more complex than I have presented them here, and go beyond the scope of this book. However, I believe they constitute the most formidable barrier to employer-supported child care and that it is absolutely necessary to begin a serious consideration of them.

Lack of Knowledge

A final barrier to child care support by employers is lack of knowledge of options. Although only 15 out of 69 employers in the Delaware Valley survey mentioned this, other studies suggest it is fairly common (Policy/Action Institute 1986).

Many companies have not been solicited about child care either from within or from without, and they are completely unfamiliar with what other employers are currently doing. Nor are they aware of the costs and benefits that accompany various options. Obviously, lack of knowledge is related to lack of demand: If employers do not hear a need expressed by their employees, it is doubtful that they are going to seek out and research another benefit to offer them.

In sum, what is common among employers who have never considered child care and those who have but opted not to provide it is the perception that, while child care may be something that would help employees, it is not necessary for the operation of their companies. Costs, liability, licensing, space, and equity issues are seen by many employers as substantial reasons not to sponsor child care.

But these concerns are also felt by employers who do decide to sponsor child care. Thus, something absent in the former cases must be operating in the latter to overcome these obstacles. This ultimately seems to be the belief by people at the top levels of the organization that the benefits of having a child care program far outweigh the risks. They can come to this conclusion only if people within the organization express their child care needs and demonstrate effectively that these have a direct effect on their productivity.

CONCLUSION

Employers identify different reasons or motivations for their involvement in the provision of child care to their employees. In many cases, they are straightforward about their need to attract and retain certain desirable employees and to offer whatever incentive they can to accomplish this. If they need young employees, particularly women of childbearing age, one of the benefits that is currently most attractive and least available from other employers is child care. It is therefore perceived to be a very effective recruitment tool.

Other employers present their motives as more altruistic. Their support of child care is presented as illustrating the extent to which they care about their employees as workers and as parents. Once they have identified that child care is a problem affecting people's home and work life, these companies feel they have an obligation to do something to help. In some cases, the company has a reputation as family oriented and caring. In others, it is the spillover of family problems into work performance that prompts the employer to institute an assistance program such as child care.

It is a rare case that employers are pushed in any way into supporting child care by demanding employees. In some cases, informal and formal requests have been effective in making the need known. In others, individuals who are in positions of power, and who have child care needs themselves, have been able to affect their companies' involvements.

In any event, evidence from employers who do choose to sponsor child care illustrates that the implementation of a new and costly program, one that ultimately serves a small proportion of the total work force, is not something companies do without a great deal of reflection. This is made clear in the descriptions of the decision-making processes among the employers I interviewed. In all cases, a good deal of research on options, comparison of existing programs, cost projections, surveys of employees, and discussions with community agencies were undertaken before company officials would consider sponsoring child care. Many levels of approval were necessary, including boards of directors (who tend to be very removed from the issue themselves, as they are generally composed of older men). What this suggests is that employers must somehow come to believe that supporting child care is in their own short or long term interests. And it suggests that each of the particular reasons to support child care offered by employers would be irrelevant if it did not fit into the larger needs and structures of contemporary work organizations, organizations that are increasingly composed of women.

However, what the process of decision making also suggests is that as long as employees at all levels hesitate to make their child care needs known, the barriers to further employer involvement will remain significant. While I have cited a few examples of executives acting upon their own child care needs, these are exceptional. The lack of recognition of employees' child care problems among most executives and administrators is profound. It is up to other employees to enlighten them.

NOTES

1. It is unclear whether there was indeed an actual shortage of nurses, and why it occurred at this particular time (1979–1980). It is possible that something was going on at the time that discouraged nurses from working in their field and contributed to a *perception* by the medical establishment of a shortage. This is the view expressed by the Institute of Medicine (1981).

Kalisch and Kalisch (1980), on the other hand, refer to a dramatic proliferation of articles in newspapers across the country attesting to a real, absolute, and national nursing shortage.

Whatever the reality, the important thing for our discussion is that medical employers at least *perceived* a shortage of nurses in 1979–1980, and that some did so to such a degree that they instituted a relatively radical recruitment program—child care.

Apparently, a new nursing shortage is emerging at the time of this writing. It will be interesting to see if more hospitals and medical centers offer child care benefits as a recruitment tool in this situation.

2. It should be mentioned that there are conflicting analyses of the measurable effects of employer-supported child care in reducing absenteeism, tardiness, and turnover, and therefore improving productivity. While Burud et al. (1984) cite cases in which positive effects were measurable, Miller (1984) cautions against uncritical acceptance of the methodology and the findings of many such cases.

3. Some employers, however, have removed the word "referral" from their child care information services for fear of being considered liable in the case of an unsatisfactory referral arrangement.

4. Roberta L. Bergman, executive director for resource develop-

ment, Child Care Dallas, Testimony, in U.S. House of Representatives, Select Committee on Children, Youth, and Families, *Child Care: Exploring Private and Public Sector Approaches* (Washington, DC: U.S. Government Printing Office, 1984), 23–24.

Chapter 5

The Significance of Employer-Supported Child Care

The United States has never had a coherent child care policy. For years it has been assumed that child care is, and should be, within the private domain of family and home. A pervasive ideology of mothering, which holds that child care is always a mother's first duty, has both limited women's occupational opportunities and limited publicly suported extrafamilial child care. Where government has been involved in child care, it has been as an agent of last resort, and has focused on poor and welfare mothers who are perceived to have failed in their duties.

But over the last two decades, social, cultural, and economic changes in the structure of families and work have converged to raise the issue of responsibility for child care to a more salient position than it has previously held. The increased labor force participation of women; the growth of traditionally female sectors of the economy; the rise in the divorce rate, resulting in an increase in the number of single-female-headed households; and the impact of feminist consciousness on the population as a whole together challenge the traditional image of family and "a woman's place."

Yet, this challenge occurs simultaneously with a growing welfare state backlash movement most strongly articulated in the tax-cutting policies and limitations on government spending for social services of the Reagan administration. With a majority of mothers working, and with funding cuts and the dissolution of government social services agencies and progams, the question is, Who is left to carry some of the responsibility for child care?

Increasingly, part of the answer seems to be employers, because they are directly affected by the instability and low productivity of employees with child care problems, because they have the capital (and some tax-based incentives) necessary for instituting a child care program in response, and because many employees think that it is time for employers to help.

We have seen from the data presented in this book that employers who become involved in providing child care do so out of their own organizational self-interest. They must come to believe that the quality, stability, and productivity of their work force is directly affected by employees' child care problems, and that it is worth their while to address these problems. But the question remains, Does their involvement in the provision of child care have larger implications than just those for their organizational needs? I would argue that indeed it does; for even though it is not (yet) widespread, employer-supported child care is significant because it *inadvertently* poses a direct challenge to the ideology of mothering, and in so doing, contributes to the potential for greater opportunities for women. It does this in two important ways. First, it positively sanctions mothers' working outside the home; and second, it positively sanctions extra-familial child care. Evidence for this interpretation comes from further comments made by the employers I interviewed.

MOTHERS WORKING

All the employers I interviewed believed that most women now work outside the home both out of need and out of choice. They pointed out that current economic and life-style standards virtually require the income of two parents to support a family. A few employers felt that to some degree our notion of "need" is a subjective reflection of life-style choices, and that individual families could choose, for example, to lower their standard of living a bit so as not to require both parents to work full-time when they have young children. But most maintained that it is unrealistic in this day and age to expect that women (not to mention men) would be either willing or able to stay home all day with their children.

At the same time, employers understood the dilemmas that

this situation produces in the relationship between parents and children, especially among mothers who still feel torn about their responsibilities to work and to family. They argued that, as much as possible, parents must decide what is the most satisfying arrangement, because children will be adversely affected by dissatisfaction. The comment of the human resources manager at New York Glass was typical:

I think so much of it depends on how both the mother and father feel about the thing. If the mother wants to be at home and she's at work, the kid's not going to be happy because she'll be communicating it. If she wants to be at work and she's at home, the kid is not going to be happy either. So, I believe that a lot of it depends upon how you feel about yourself; you have to be where you want to be. Now, the overriding problem with this is that a lot of people don't have that choice. If you look at the data, you know that women have to work whether they want to or not. And that's when things get complicated, because those people who have to go to work may resent the fact that they do, and this makes it more difficult for the kid.

The language of this employer suggests that it is not only the mother who must work out this dilemma. In fact, one of the most surprising revelations in this study was that employers in general approached the question of appropriate work and child care arrangements as a *parents'*, not a *woman's*, issue. This is not to say that they believed that fathers are participating in child care responsibilities on an equal basis with mothers. Rather, they felt that we as a society must begin to see child care as an issue that affects both parents, especially when both are working. This sentiment was expressed in the following comment from the benefits administrator at Island Fruit:

A person who needs to work, needs to work, regardless of outside extracurricular activities, regardless of gender, regardless of whether you have young children, old children, are starting a family, or not. So I don't differentiate between a male or female in the same situation; there shouldn't be any difference. I feel that child care is as important to the fathers as it is to the mothers. Certainly there are a lot of single parents, and a majority of them are mothers—I won't argue that fact—but a single parent father has the same problem the single parent mother does. I'll also say that many parents give the responsibility for the child to the mother, in that even if there are two parents, the mother's the one who's doing everything. While that's the trend, there's a large percent of families that do not share that particular stereotype. I think that the issue of child care is a real *parent* problem.

The notion that child care is a working parent's concern carried over into employers' discussions of what they thought was the ideal care situation for young children. Surprisingly, only 2 of the 25 employers I interviewed specified that a mother's staying home and taking care of her young child is the best situation (and even in these cases, they were only talking about children under 18 months old). The consensus among all the other employers was that the ideal care situation is one that is worked out between parents, with which they are comfortable, and which involves a consistent care giver who can provide love, nourishment, and engagement to the child. This consistent care giver need not be the child's mother or father, but can also be another relative, a friend, or a professional. Whatever the choice, it is the responsibility of the parent to ensure that consistent care is found. As the vice-president for human resources at Southern Financial put it:

I don't think the parent ever gives up the responsibility for the care of the child. I think it's the responsibility of the parent, if the parent chooses to enter the work force, to make sure that the parent is selecting a quality caregiver. I don't think that, just by virtue of the fact that someone is a mother or a father to a child biologically, that makes them a good parent.

A similar comment came from the vice-president of Western Financial Foundation (a company not previously discussed here):

I think parents need to put together the best set of arrangements for their child's upbringing and welfare that they possibly can. That's in my mind their primary responsibility as parents. If we talk about child care out of the home, it's part of a patchwork of care that a child gets. Maybe it's a little piece of the quilt, or maybe it's most of it, or it varies depending on the age of the child, the time of year, or whatever. But, if the parent feels that there is outside care that they are comfortable with, that blends with their parenting style, and that they think their child feels very comfortable with, then I see no problem incorporating it into the overall structure of care that a child gets.

These comments suggest that these employers differentiate between the responsibility for child care and the act of child care. Both are significant, but it is no longer necessary that they belong to the same person—the mother. Responsibility for the care situation of children always lies with parents—mother and father, if present—but they may choose to delegate the actual tasks to someone else during the day. This attitude suggests that these employers accept the reality of working mothers by asserting that child care arrangements must be something worked out by negotiation between two parents, both of whom have nonfamily obligations and commitments, not something automatically assigned by sex. It also suggests that they recognize that an increasing number of famililes do not have two parents, and the women heading these families must work to support them.

EXTRAFAMILIAL CHILD CARE

In acknowledging that it is appropriate for mothers to work, these employers can also be seen as supporting the idea that it is therefore appropriate for someone besides the mother to take care of her children during the day. In the course of my interviews with them, it became clear that many employers viewed child care as a social, not just a private family, problem. They argued that the effects of bad care can be felt at all levels of society—the schools, the criminal justice system, and work organizations. Therefore, they asserted, if parents are not able to provide the best care possible for their children, they have a social responsibility to delegate those tasks to someone who can; and at the same time, society has a responsibility to make sure that those people exist.

One of the most provocative comments made by a number of employers in this regard was that parents in many cases may not be the best people to be taking care of their children in this day and age. The employers who said this seemed to be responding to a few things. First was their concern that working parents simply do not have the time or energy to give the proper attention and care to their children. Second, these employers were reacting to increasing reports of child abuse within families and in formal and informal child care settings. And third, since these employers were sponsoring professional programs, they had adopted a professionalized attitude about what appropriate child care is. Many subscribed to child development models asserting that young children need a certain quality, not just quantity, of care to ensure their proper physical, emotional, intellectual, and social development. Employers who sponsored a child care center in particular felt that their programs provide that kind of care, while many parents do not. The comments of the director of Southern Catholic Hospital typified this perspective:

There are a lot of children who would be in bad shape if they were home with their parents. There are a lot of children who are better off here, because you can see parents' reactions to their children, their lack of interest in the children. I think that one of our advantages is the child development training. Actually, we probably do more with the child than the parent, except maybe in the amount of time that can be spent with them on an individual basis. But I think you'd find that most mothers at home with their children do not spend much time interacting with them. They're doing the laundry, and cooking, and watching T.V., and cleaning the house; and probably, if it came right down to it, they spend about the same amount of time with them really on a one-to-one basis as they would after they get the children home from day care.

While a comment such as this might be expected from a child care center director, others like it reflect the winning over of an employer, as in this comment from the vice-president of human resources at Community Hospital, who had four adult children:

I think that the child care center has a good curriculum; a program. All you have to do is go over there and see them in operation, and see babies stretching to exercise their muscles—little things they do that you don't even think of when you're at home. The thing that comes to mind after raising four children is that nobody gives a class on parenting—at least they didn't in my day. And I think that's very important because, for example, the kids that get the kind of care our center offers from infant to school age are getting something that a lot of kids, including mine, didn't get.

For some employers, the quality of their child care program goes beyond curriculum. It is not just the children who benefit from the program, but parents as well who, by participating in it, are assisted in both their work and their family responsibilities and are given support to develop in both areas:

Our idea of quality is providing a service to each of our families and each of our children, where care is given in such a way that we know what happens to a child each day. And, at the same time, we're helping the parent and working with the parent—not just in an academic sense—but also providing opportunities for them to be independent, for them to be thinking, for helping them to develop skills for coping with life and with their families. We can all work together; we're not a substitute for a family unit, but we're part of it. Since the parent has to go to work, we're there for support. (Director, Southwest Engineering)

An additional benefit of an employer-supported on-site child care center mentioned by the director of Southwest Engineering's program is its ability to demystify the world of work for children:

[An on-site center] serves to not isolate the child from the world of work that is so much a part of his life—that has become a part of his life, and will become a part of his life. Because children traditionally see work as taking their parents away from them, and there's a whole world that they don't understand, they cast it as "the bad guy." They think "if you didn't have to work you could stay home with me and take me to the movies." These children get to see work in a positive way. Work is a way of earning money so that you can purchase things and do things and make everyone happy. Work is also a place where you get to see your mommy, or meet your daddy's friend. Work is also a place where parents get to show off their children and to include them in their whole world.

From this and the previous comments, we can see that for many employers the provision of extrafamilial child care, far from being a dangerous phenomenon, is a positive one for children, parents, and society. While many might not have believed this previous to their company's involvement, the establishment of a child care program—especially one of quality—proved to be very convincing.

CONCLUSION

In sum, the involvement of these employers is significant because, even as an unintended consequence, it represents an *institutional* expression of both the acceptance of mothers' working and the acceptance of extrafamilial child care. This may seem to be an overly optimistic conclusion, especially as it is based on a few thousand "model" employers and it depends upon continued involvement by more. But I would argue that this commitment is forthcoming, because these organizations now realize that the problems raised by a *lack* of attention to child care needs affect them directly—whether by reduced employee productivity or by child abuse and neglect.

However, it cannot be up to employers alone. What is clearly needed is a growth in cooperative ventures involving employers, governments, unions, and local community organizations. For it is unlikely that all companies will come to see offering child care as in their self-interest; and it is therefore dangerous to have such great expectations of them. Indeed, particularly in earlier years, a number of employer-supported child care centers closed once companies no longer saw them as necessary or effective in recruiting, retaining, or improving employee morale relative to their cost. (Some of this may have been a result of a company's choosing to operate a center rather than offering other options. Both the cost and the "fit" with employees' needs may have been inaccurately anticipated.)[1]

Furthermore, some on- or near-site child care centers are too expensive for many employees who perhaps need them the most—low wage, lower level workers. Where this is the case, it heightens the potential for the maintenance of a class-stratified child care system, in which those with money have access to good child care and those without do not. Yet employers cannot be expected to fully subsidize child care for all their employees who need it. They simply will not do it, nor do many people think the ought to.

But governments and communities can. Clearly, child care is not just an employer's concern. Child care is a societal concern. Children are members of communities as well as of families; they are future citizens as much as they are future workers, and therefore we all have a stake in their well-being.[2] At the same time, we all have a stake in the well-being of parents. It is not just employers', but also governments' and the public's, obligation to create environments that contribute to the physical, emotional, and social well-being of all. The conflicts that parents—especially women—face in trying to balance competing commitments to work and family life are real. The dilemma of child care is perhaps the greatest source of such conflict, but it is one that is not completely insurmountable if all resources are put to creative use.

Thus, we must view employer-supported child care as only a partial solution to a salient social problem. Whether one sees it as symbolic, because only a small number of companies are so far involved, or as real, because an increasing number are becoming involved, employer-supported child care signifies a recognition that family life and work life have changed, that they are no longer separable as aspects of working parents' lives, and that new arrangements must be made to accommodate those changes. Their involvement is an important part of an inevitable extension of extrafamilial child care as one of those new arrangements. In fact, I think it is really only a first step toward a wider reorganization of both family life and work life to accommodate a range of choices parents want to make, including whether to work full-time. Its significance lies in making those choices available to women as well as to men.

NOTES

1. For an example of one company that closed an on-site child care center—AT&T—see Kahn and Kamerman (1987:178–179).

2. A few communities, recognizing this, have passed legislation intended to have the effect of bolstering community child care resources. The San Francisco Board of Supervisors, for example, passed a city ordinance in 1985 requiring developers of new downtown commercial property of 50,000 square feet or more to provide on-site child care facilities or to contribute a dollar per square foot to a city-run fund established to enhance and extend community-based child care programs. Concord, California, has a similar ordinance, and other cities are considering doing the same.

Appendix:

A Note on Unions

Overall, unions have played a very minor role in child care—including employer-supported child care—and it is doubtful that they will become more involved in the future, Nevertheless, their recent activity is worth noting here.

As part of the general emphasis on child development in the 1960s, the AFL-CIO declared "its wholeharted support for programs which strengthen and safeguard family life and help to assure each child the fullest healthy mental and physical development" (Creque 1979). Regarding child care specifically, that support has taken two forms: lobbying for federal and state legislation, and collective bargaining with employers and community agencies. Under the 1969 amendment to the Taft-Hartley Act, unions can use child care as a negotiable item much like health insurance pensions.

Yet, regardless of unions' stated commitment, a Bureau of National Affairs (1984) survey of ten major unions found only one case in which child care funding has been secured through private sector collective bargaining arrangements: by the Amalgamated Clothing and Textile Workers Union (ACTWU). It is no coincidence that this is a union with a predominantly female membership. According to Bobbie Creque, a vice-president of ACTWU and chair of the Coalition of Labor Union Women, in order for greater union interest and support to appear, child care will have to be removed from the realm of "women's issues" (1979).

A move in that direction occurred when, at its 1983 convention, the AFL-CIO adopted a resolution calling for both national and international unions to emphasize child care "as a vitally important bargaining issue." While substantive agreements and programs are still lacking, child care is now part of the bargaining programs of several unions, including the United Automobile Workers, the Newspaper Guild, Service Employees International Union, the Communications Workers of America, and the American Federation of Government Employees. In most cases, activity has centered on contract proposals and feasibility studies; and where centers have been recommended, they have not been adopted. Even proposals for alternative work schedules to assist working parents with child care arrangements have been resisted by unions (such as the American Federation of State, County and Municipal Employees) that are concerned about running the risk of circumventing the intent of contracts (Anderson 1983).

Aside from lobbying and collective bargaining efforts, a few unions have directly supported child care centers. These include the Seafarers International Union in Ponce, Puerto Rico, which ran a one-year pilot program in 1973, and the United Federation of Teachers, Local 2, of New York, which at one time operated 20 centers but had to close them during the state's financial crisis in 1972 (Creque 1979).

But the most prominent example of direct union involvement is the ACTWU, which sponsored six child care centers for its members in the Mid-Atlantic region, beginning in 1968. By 1977, ACTWU may have been the largest nonprofit provider of day care services in the United States. But between 1977 and 1986, failures in the apparel industry resulted in the closing of most of these centers.

Currently, the International Ladies Garment Workers Union (ILGWU) is involved in a child care center in New York City's Chinatown district. However, the union contributes nothing financially. Rather, the center is supported with public and private funding (it also had start-up funding from management) and is available to low wage ILGWU members who qualify for public child care assistance. Needless to say, this is a unique arrangement.

Indeed, the more common experience of ACTWU and the other unions points to two significant limitations to union activity in child care. The first is the availability of funds. While collective bargaining contracts are one potential source, they are not necessarily the most advantageous one for unions. On the whole, union members historically have preferred that collective bargaining money go to wage increases for all members, rather than to a program, such as child care, that is seen to benefit only a few (Anderson 1983; Bureau of National Affairs 1984). An alternative approach is to have the union lobby for funds for child care from state legislatures, as did the National Union of Hospital and Health Care employees in Connecticut, which succeeded in obtaining funds after a labor-management study determined that real need existed (Bureau of National Affairs 1984). But we know that unless long-term commitment accompanies that funding—from legislatures or from employers—child care programs are vulnerable to closure, as happened to that of New York City's United Federation of Teachers.

The second limitation to unions' involvement in child care has to do with the level of union organization. Whether or not it should, child care remains primarily a woman's issue. Many women now work in industries and work places that are not union organized, and therefore they do not have the kind of bargaining power that they might need to involve employers in child care on their behalf. This, of course, occurs in the context of declining union membership nationally. Dana Friedman (1983c) says:

Unions are losing membership largely because they are concentrated in the older, dying industries. Until recently, they have not focused on the technical workers, white-collar workers or women—the three fastest growing groups of employees—as well as those working in our growth industries. Therefore, little pressure for family benefits has been exerted by the unions or prompted by management in unionized companies. . . . The lack of pressure from the union is also attributable to a 20 percent female union membership. The male-dominated union leadership and rank and file have not pushed for child care concessions at the bargaining table (p. 23).

This situation rings particularly true for working mothers who need child care the most—those in low or unskilled service sector jobs in which pay is kept low partly beause there is no union representation. Without the support of unions, there is no institutional mechanism for establishing new programs or for enforcing maintenance of existing child care programs if they are perceived not to be cost effective, or if the need for certain workers diminishes. This was evident after World War II, when unions refused to initiate bargaining to retain women workers and to retain the child care centers established in defense industries (see Chapter 2).

In the absence of an institutional organization to initiate demand for new programs, workers must depend on the possibility that their employer will decide that it is in the company's best interest—however that is defined—to support child care.

In her 1983 study of employer initiatives for working parents in New York City, Kristin Anderson found very little support for child care from unions. Of the five unions she interviewed, only one had an "active interest" in an on- or near-site child care center; the other four had "no current interest." Only one union had an "active interest" in flexible benefits plans; the other four had "no current interest." None of the five unions was interested in dependent care subsidies or information and referral services. The only union programs in operation were two employee seminars and one flex-time work schedule. If this city's experience is any indication of others', we can assume that union interest, much less involvement, in child care will remain minimal.

Bibliography

Adams, Carolyn T., and Kathryn T. Winston. 1980. *Mothers at work: Public policies in the U.S., Sweden and China.* New York: Longman.

Ambert, Anne-Marie. 1986. Sociology of sociology: The place of children in North American sociology. In *Sociological studies of child development,* Vol. 1, edited by P. Adler and P. A. Adler, 11–31. Greenwich, Connecticut: JAI Press.

Anderson, Karen, 1981. *Wartime women: Sex roles, family relations and the status of women during World War II.* Westport, Connecticut: Greenwood Press.

Anderson, Kristin, 1983. *Corporate initiatives for working parents in New York City: A ten-industry review.* New York: Center for Public Advocacy Research.

Angrist, Shirley S., Judith R. Lave, and Richard Mickelson. 1976. How working mothers manage: Socioeconomic differences in work, child care and household tasks. *Social Science Quarterly* 56:631–637.

Aries, Philippe. 1962. *Centuries of childhood: A social history of family life.* Translated from the French by Robert Baldick. New York: Vintage Books.

Auerbach, Judith D. 1986. Working parents and child care responsibility in the U.S.: The new role of the employer. Ph.D. dissertation, University of California, Berkeley.

—— 1987. Child care responsibility as a barrier to women's achievement of the American Dream: How employers may make a difference. Paper presented at the annual meeting of the Eastern Sociological Society, Boston.

Auerbach, Steveanne. 1979. *Confronting the child care crisis.* Boston: Beacon Press.

Baden, Clifford, and Dana E. Friedman, eds. 1981. *New management initiatives for working parents.* Reports from an April 1981 conference. Boston: Wheelock College.

Baden, Ruth Kramer, Andrea Genser, James A. Levine, and Michelle Seligson. 1982. *School-age child care: An action manual.* Boston, Massachusetts: Auburn House.

Badinter, Elisabeth. 1980. *Mother love: Myth and reality.* New York: Macmillan.

Bane, Mary Jo. 1976. *Here to stay: American families in the twentieth century.* New York: Basic Books.

Bane, Mary Jo, Laura Lein, Lydia O'Donnell, C. Ann Stueve, and Barbara Wells. 1979. Child care arrangements of working parents. *Monthly Labor Review* 102 (October):50–56.

Beck, Rochelle. 1982. Beyond the stalemate in child care public policy. In *Day care: Scientific and social policy issues,* edited by Edward F. Zigler and Edmund W. Gordon, 307–337. Boston: Auburn House.

Belsky, Jay, and Laurence D. Steinberg. 1978. The effects of day care: A critical review. *Child Development* 49:929–949.

Berger, Brigitte, and Peter L. Berger. 1983. *The war over the family: Capturing the middle ground.* New York: Anchor Press/Doubleday.

Blank, Helen. 1984. *Child care: The states' response, A survey of state child care policies 1983–1984.* Washington, D.C.: Children's Defense Fund.

Blank, Helen, and Amy Wilkins. 1985. *Child care: Whose priority? A state child care fact book 1985.* Washington, D.C.: Children's Defense Fund.

Blood, Robert O., Jr., and Donald M. Wolfe. 1960. *Husbands and wives: The dynamics of married living.* Glencoe, Illinois: The Free Press.

Bloom, Benjamin S. 1964. *Stabililty and change in human characteristics.* New York: Wiley.

Bohen, Halcyone H., and Anamaria Viveros-Long. 1981. *Balancing jobs and family life.* Philadelphia: Temple University Press.

Boles, Janet K. 1980. The politics of child care. *Social Service Review* 3 (September):344–362.

Bourne, Patricia Gerald. 1972. What day care ought to be. *The New Republic* 166 (February 12):18–23.

Bowlby, John. 1952. *Maternal care and mental health.* Geneva: World Health Organization.

Brandwein, Ruth, Carol Brown, and Elizabeth Maury Fox. 1974. Women and children last: The social situation of divorced mothers and their families. *Journal of Marriage and the Family* 36:498–514.

Bremner, R. H. 1971. *Children and youth in America: A documentary history*, Vol. 2, *1866–1932*. Cambridge, Massachusetts: Harvard University Press.

Bureau of National Affairs. 1984. *Employers and child care: Development of a new employee benefit*. Washington, D.C.: Bureau of National Affairs.

Burud, Sandra L., Pamela R. Aschbacher,and Jacquelyn M. Mc-Croskey. 1984. *Employer supported child care: Investing in human resources*. Boston: Auburn House.

Business Week. 1943. Women drop out. (August 21):88–89.

———. 1981. Child care grows as a benefit.(December 21):60–61.

Canon, Belle. 1978. Child care where you work. *Ms.* (April):83–86.

Catalyst. 1983. Child care information services: An option for employer support of child care. Position paper RR #7. New York: Catalyst.

Chafe, William Henry. 1972. *The American woman: Her changing social, economic, and political roles, 1920–1970*. New York: Oxford University Press.

Child Care Coordinating Council of San Mateo. No Date. Parents in the workforce. San Mateo, California: Child Care Coordinating Council.

Chodorow, Nancy. 1978. *The reproduction of mothering*. Berkeley: University of California Press.

Chodorow, Nancy, and Susan Contratto. 1982. The fantasy of the perfect mother. In *Rethinking the family: Some feminist questions*, edited by Barrie Thorne and Marilyn Yalom. New York: Longman.

Clarke-Stewart, Alison. 1977. *Child care in the family: A review of research and some propositions for policy*. New York: Academic Press.

———. 1982. *Daycare*. Cambridge, Massachusetts: Harvard University Press.

Commerce Clearing House. 1982. *Tax incentives for employer-sponsored child care programs*. Chicago: Commerce Clearing House.

The Conference Board. 1985. Update on employer-supported child care initiatives. Prepared by Dana E. Friedman. New York: The Conference Board.

Cook, Alice H. 1975. *The working mother: A survey of problems and pro-*

grams in nine countries. Ithaca, New York: State School of Industrial and Labor Relations, Cornell University.

Creque, Bobbie. 1979. Labor and child care. Alexandria, Virginia: United Way of America.

Dalla Costa, Mariarosa, and Selma James. 1972. *The power of women and the subversion of the community*. Bristol, England: Falling Wall Press.

Dally Ann. 1982. *Inventing motherhood: The consequences of an ideal*. New York: Schocken Books.

Davidoff, Lenore. 1976. The rationalization of housework. In *Dependence and exploitation in work and marriage*, edited by Diana Leonard Barker and Sheila Allen, 121–151. London: Longman.

Dinnerstein, Dorothy. 1976. *The mermaid and the minotaur: Sexual arrangements and human malaise*. New York: Harper and Row.

Dratch, Howard. 1974. The politics of child care in the 1940s. *Science and Society* (Summer):167–204.

Ericksen, Julia A., William L. Yancey, and Eugene P. Ericksen. 1979. The division of family roles. *Journal of Marriage and the Family* 41 (May):301–313.

Feinstein, Karen Wolk. 1979. Directions for day care. In *Working women and families*, edited by Karen Wolk Feinstein. Beverly Hills, California: Sage.

Fernandez, Happy, and Jessica deGroot. 1986. An investigation into day care in Philadelphia. Philadelphia: School of Social Administration, Temple University.

Fernandez, John P. 1986. *Child care and corporate productivity: Resolving family/work conflicts*. Lexington, Massachusetts: Lexington Books.

Floge, Liliane. 1985. The dynamics of child care use and some implications for women's employment. *Journal of Marriage and the Family* 47:143–154.

Fraiberg, Selma. 1977. *Every child's birthright: In defense of mothering*. New York: Basic Books.

Frank, Miriam, Marilyn Zeibarth, and Connie Field. 1982. *The life and times of Rosie the Riveter*. Emeryville, California: Clarity Educational Productions.

Friedman, Dana E. 1981. Child care in the 80s: Reaching out to business and labor. Reprint #9, Employers and child care. Belmont, Massachusetts: Child Care Information Exchange.

———. 1983a. Employer supported child care: How does it answer the needs of workers? *Vital Issues* 32, 10:1–6.

———. 1983b. *Government initiatives to encourage employer supported child care: The state and local perspective.* New York: Center for Public Advocacy Research.

————. 1983c. Encouraging employer support to working parents: Community strategies for change. A report of the Working Parents Project for Carnegie Corporation of New York. New York: Center for Public Advocacy Research.

————. 1985. *Corporate financial assistance for child care.* Work and Family Information Center, Research Bulletin no. 177. New York: The Conference Board.

Gardiner, Jean. 1976. Political economy of domestic labor in capitalist society. In *Dependence and exploitation in work and marriage,* edited by Diana Leonard Barker and Sheila Allen, 109–120. London: Longman.

General Mills, Inc. 1981. *Families at work: Strengths and strains. The General Mills American family report.* Conducted by Louis Harris and Associates. Minneapolis: General Mills, Inc.

Gerald, Patricia. 1972. The three faces of day care. In *The future of the family,* edited by Louise Kapp Howe, 268–282. New York: Simon and Schuster.

Gerson, Kathleen. 1986. *Hard choices: How women decide about work, career, and motherhood.* Berkeley, California: University of California Press.

Gilligan, Carol. 1982. *In a different voice: Psychological theory and women's development.* Cambridge, Massachusetts: Harvard University Press.

Glick, Paul C. 1984. American household structure in transition. *Family Planning Perspectives* 16 (September/October):205–211.

Goldman, Karla Shepard, and Michael Lewis. 1976. *Child care and public policy: A case study.* Princeton, New Jersey: Educational Testing Service, Institute for Research in Human Development.

Governor's Advisory Committee on Child Development. 1981. *Employer sponsored child care.* Sacramento, California: Governor's Advisory Committee on Child Development.

Greenblatt, Bernard. 1977. *Responsibililty for child care.* San Francisco: Jossey-Bass.

Gregory, Chester W. 1974. *Women in defense work during World War II: An analysis of the labor problem and women's rights.* New York: Exposition Press.

Grubb, W. Norton, and Marvin Lazerson. 1982. *Broken promises: How Americans fail their children.* New York: Basic Books.

Hagen, E. 1975. Child care and women's liberation. In *Child Care— who cares? Foreign and domestic infant and early childhood develop-*

ment policies, edited by Pamela Roby, 284–296. New York: Basic Books.

Harrell, J. E., and C. A. Ridley. 1975. Substitute child care, maternal employment and the quality of mother-child interaction. *Journal of Marriage and the Family* 37:556–564.

Hartmann, Heidi. 1981. The family as the locus of gender, class and political struggle: The example of housework. *Signs* 6 (Spring):366–394.

Hartmann, Susan M. 1982. *The homefront and beyond: American women in the 1940s.* Boston: Twayne Publishers.

Hertz, Rosanna. 1986. *More equal than others: Women and men in dual career marriages.* Berkeley: University of California Press.

Hewitt Associates. 1982. Child care assistance: Issues for employer consideration. Lincolnshire, Illinois: Hewitt Associates.

Hewlett, Sylvia. 1986. *A lesser life: The myth of women's liberation in America.* New York: William Morrow.

Hofferth, Sandra L. 1979. Day care in the next decade: 1980–1990. *Journal of Marriage and the Family* 41 (August):649–657.

Hoffman, Lois Wladis. 1963. Parental power relations and the division of household tasks. In *The employed mother in America*, edited by F. Ivan Howe and Lois Wladis Hoffman. Chicago: Rand McNally.

Honey, Maureen. 1984. *Creating Rosie the Riveter: Class, gender, and propaganda during World War II.* Amherst: University of Massachusetts Press.

Immerwahr, John. 1984. Building a consensus on the child care problem. *Personal Administrator* (February):31–37.

Institute of Medicine. 1981. *Six-month interim report by the committee of the Institute of Medicine for a study of nursing and nursing education.* Washington, D.C.: National Academy Press.

Joffe, Carole. 1972. Child care: Destroying the family or strengthening it? In *The future of the family*, edited by Louise Kapp Howe, 261–267. New York: Simon and Schuster.

———. 1977. *Friendly intruders: Childcare professionals and family life.* Berkeley: University of California Press.

Kahn, Alfred J., and Sheila B. Kamerman. 1987. *Child care: Facing the hard choices.* Dover, Massachusetts: Auburn House.

Kalisch, Philip A., and Beatrice J. Kalish. 1980. The nursing shortage, the president, and the congress. *Nursing Forum* 19:138-164.

Kamerman, Sheila B. 1980. *Parenting in an unresponsive society.* New York: The Free Press.

Kamerman, Sheila B., and Alfred J. Kahn. 1978. *Family policy: Govern-*

ment and families in fourteen countries. New York: Columbia University Press.

———. 1979. The day care debate. A wider view. *The Public Interest* 54 (Winter):76–93.

———. 1981. *Child care, family benefits, and working parents: A study in comparative policy.* New York: Columbia University Press.

Kamerman, Sheila B., and C. D. Hayes, eds. 1982. *Families that work: Children in a changing world.* Washington, D.C.: National Academy Press.

Kanter, Rosabeth Moss. 1977. *Men and women of the corporation.* New York: Basic Books.

———. 1983. *The change masters: Innovation and entrepreneurship in the American corporation.* New York: Simon and Schuster.

Kerr, Virginia. 1973. One step forward—two steps back: Child care's long American history. In *Child care—who cares? Foreign and domestic infant and early childhood development policies,* edited by Pamela Roby, 151–171. New York: Basic Books.

Kessler-Harris, Alice. 1982. *Out to work: A history of wage-earning women in the United States.* New York: Oxford University Press.

Keyserling, Mary. 1972. *Windows on day care.* New York: National Council of Jewish Women.

Krucoff, Carol. 1980. Corporate solutions in on-site day care. *Los Angeles Times,* July 27, Part 7:9.

Lasch, Christopher.1977. *Haven in a heartless world.* New York: Basic Books.

Lenz, Elinor, and Barbara Myerhoff. 1985. *The feminization of America: How women's values are changing our public and private lives.* Los Angeles: Jeremy P. Tarcher.

Lopata, Helen Znaniecka. 1971. *Occupation: Housewife.* New York: Oxford University Press.

Lopata, Helen Znaniecka, with Cheryl Allyn Miller and Debra Barnewolt. 1984. *City women: Work, jobs, occupations, careers,* Vol. 1, *America.* New York: Praeger.

Low, Seth, and Pearl Spindler. 1968. Child care arrangements of working mothers in the U.S. Children's Bureau Publication no. 461. Washington, D.C.: U.S. Department of Health, Education and Welfare.

Lowenberg, Miriam E. 1944. Shipyard nursery schools. *Journal of Home Economics* 36 (February): 75–77.

Lublin, Joann B. 1981. The new interest in corporate day care. *The Wall Street Journal,* April 20:18.

Magid, Renee Y. 1983. *Child care initiatives for working parents: Why em-*

ployers get involved. New York: American Management Association.

Margolis, Maxine L. 1984. *Mothers and such: Views of American women and why they changed.* Berkeley: University of California Press.

Masnick, George, and Mary Jo Bane. 1980. *The nation's families, 1960–1990.* Boston: Auburn House.

Meade, Marion. 1971. The politics of day care. *Commonweal* (April 16):133–135.

Meyer, Pearl. 1978. Women executives are different. In *Women in management,* edited by Bette Ann Stead. Englewood Cliffs, New Jersey: Prentice-Hall.

Milkman, Ruth. 1987. *Gender and work: the dynamics of job segregation by sex during World War II.* Urbana: University of Illinois Press.

Miller, Thomas I. 1984. The effects of employer-sponsored child care on employee absenteeism, turnover, productivity, recruitment or job satisfaction: What is claimed and what is known. *Personnel Psychology* 37:277–289.

Moore, Kristin A., and Isabel V. Sawhill. 1978. Implications of women's employment for home and family life. In *Women working: Theories and facts in perspective,* edited by Ann H. Stromberg and Shirley Harkess. Palo Alto, California: Mayfield.

Murray, Kathleen A. 1981. Legal aspects of child care as an employee benefit. San Francisco: The Bay Area Child Care Law Project.

National Employer Supported Child Care Project. 1982. List of employer supported child care programs in the U.S., 1981–1982. Pasadena, California: Child Care Information Service.

National Manpower Council. 1957. *Womanpower.* New York: Columbia University Press.

Newsweek. 1984. What price day care? (September 10):14–21.

Oakley, Ann. 1974a. *The sociology of housework.* New York: Pantheon.

————. 1974b. *Women's work: The housewife past and present.* New York: Vintage Books.

O'Connell, Martin, and David E. Bloom. 1987. Juggling jobs and babies: America's child care challenge. *Population trends and public policy* no. 12. Washington, D.C.: Population Reference Bureau.

Parents in the Workplace. 1983. *Sick child care.* Minneapolis: Greater Minneapolis Day Care Association.

Parsons, Talcott, and Robert F. Bales. 1955. *Family, socialization and interaction process.* Glencoe, Illinois: The Free Press.

Perry, Kathryn Senn. 1978. Survey and analysis of employer-sponsored day care in the U.S. Ph.D. dissertation, University of Wisconsin, Milwaukee.

————. 1980. Child care centers sponsored by employers and labor unions in the United States. Washington, D.C.: Women's Bureau, U.S. Department of Labor.

Piven, Frances Fox, and Richard A. Cloward. 1982. *The new class war: Reagan's attack on the welfare state and its consequences.* New York: Pantheon.

Pleck, Joseph. 1985. *Working wives, working husbands.* Beverly Hills, California: Sage.

Polatnick, Margaret. 1974. Why men don't rear children. *Berkeley Journal of Sociology* 18:45–86.

Policy/Action Institute. 1986. Corporate child care initiatives: The potential for employer involvement in child care programs. Massachusetts: The Policy/Action Institute of Transitional Employment Enterprises.

Presser, Harriet B., and Wendy Baldwin. 1980. Child care as a constraint on employment: Prevalence, correlates, and bearing on the work and fertility nexus. *American Journal of Sociology* 85:1202–1213.

Rivlin, Catherine A. 1983. The corporate role in the not-so-great society. *California Management Review* 25 (Summer):151–159.

Roby, Pamela, ed. 1973. *Child care—who cares? Foreign and domestic infant and early child development policies.* New York: Basic Books.

Roland, Alan, and Barbara Harris, eds. 1979. *Career and motherhood: Struggles for a new identity.* New York: Human Services Press.

Roth, William. 1980. Day care: A spectrum of issues and policy options. *Journal of Sociology and Social Welfare* 7 (March):188–202.

Rowe, Mary Potter. 1977. Child care for the 1980s: Traditional sex roles or androgyny? In *Women into wives: The legal and economic impact of marriage,* edited by Jane Roberts Chapman and Margaret Gates, 169–193. Beverly Hills, California: Sage.

Rubin, Lillian B. 1983. *Intimate strangers: Men and women together.* New York: Harper and Row.

Ruderman, Florence A. 1968. *Child care and working mothers: A study of arrangements made for daytime care of children.* New York: Child Welfare League of America.

Ruopp, Richard R., and Jeffrey Travers. 1982. Janus faces day care: Perspectives in quality and cost. In *Day Care: Scientific and social policy issues,* edited by Edward F. Zigler and Edmund W. Gordon. Boston: Auburn House.

Rupp, Leila J. 1978. *Mobilizing women for war: German and American propaganda, 1939–1945.* Princeton, New Jersey: Princeton University Press.

Russo, Nancy Felipe. 1979. Overview: Sex roles, fertility, and the motherhood mandate. *Psychology of Women Quarterly* (Fall):7–15.

Rutter, Michael. 1982. Social-emotional consequences of day care for preschool children. In *Day care: Scientific and social policy issues,* edited by Edward F. Zigler and Edmund W. Gordon. Boston: Auburn House.

Santa Cruz County Children's Commission. 1981. Employer sponsored child care: A resource guide to child care benefit plans. Santa Cruz, California: Santa Cruz County Children's Commission.

Saraceno, Chiara. 1984. The social construction of childhood: Child care and education policies in Italy and the United States. *Social Problems 31:351–363.*

Scarr, Sandra. 1984. *Mother care: Other care.* New York: Basic Books.

Shorter, Edward. 1975. *The making of the modern family.* New York: Basic Books.

Sidel, Ruth. 1986. *Women and children last: The plight of poor women in affluent America.* New York: Viking.

Silverstein, Louise. 1981 (1977). A critical review of current research on infant day care. In *Child care, family benefits,and working parents: A study in comparative policy,* edited by Sheila B. Kamerman and Alfred J. Kahn, 265–315. New York: Columbia University Press.

Sokoloff, Natalie J. 1980. *Between money and love: The dialectics of women's home and market work.* New York: Praeger.

Sponseller, Doris Bergen, and Joel S. Fink. 1982. Public policy toward children: Identifying the problems. *Annals of the American Academy of Political and Social Science* 461:14-20.

Stacey, Judith, and Barrie Thorne. 1985. The missing feminist revolution in sociology. *Social Problems* 32:301–316.

Stead, Bette Ann. 1978. Women's contribution to management thought. In *Women in management,* edited by Bette Ann Stead. Englewood Cliffs, New Jersey: Prentice-Hall.

Stein, Susan. 1973. The company cares for children. In *Child care— who cares? Foreign and domestic infant and early child development policies,* edited by Pamela Roby, 245–261. New York: Basic Books.

Steiner, Gilbert Y. 1976. *The children's cause.* Washington, D.C.: Brookings Institution.

———. 1981. *The futility of family policy.* Washington, D.C.: Brookings Institution.

Steinfels, Margaret O'Brien. 1973. *Who's minding the children? The his-*

tory and politics of day care in America. New York: Simon and Schuster.

Stone, Lawrence. 1979. *The family, sex and marriage in England: 1500–1800*, abridged edition. New York: Harper and Row.

Suransky, Valerie Polakow. 1982. *The erosion of childhood.* Chicago: University of Chicago Press.

Thorne, Barrie. 1987. Re-visioning women and social change: Where are the children? *Gender and Society* 1:85–109.

Tobias, Sheila, and Lisa Anderson. 1973. Whatever happened to Rosie the Riveter? *Ms.* (June):92-94.

———. 1977. *What really happened to Rosie the Riveter: Demobilization and the female labor force, 1944-1947.* New York: Pantheon Books.

U.S. Bureau of the Census. 1982. Child support and alimony: 1981. Current population reports, special studies, series P-23, no. 124 (advanced report). Washington, D.C.: U.S. Government Printing Office.

———. 1983a. Child care arrangements of working mothers: June 1982. Current population reports, series P-23, no. 129. Washington, D.C.: U.S. Government Printing Office.

———. 1983b. Population profile of the U.S.: 1982. Current population reports, series P-23, no. 130. Washington, D.C.: U.S. Government Printing Office.

———. 1985a. Characteristics of the population below the poverty level: 1983. Current population reports, series P-60, no. 147. Washington, D.C.: U.S. Government Printing Office.

———. 1985b. Money income of households, families, and persons in the United States: 1983. Current population reports, series P-60, no. 146. Washington, D.C.: U.S. Government Printing Office.

———. 1986. Fertility of American women, June 1985. Current population reports, series P-20,no. 406. Washington, D.C.: U.S. Government Printing Office.

U.S. Commission on Civil Rights. 1981. Child care and equal opportunity for women. Clearinghouse publication no. 67. Washington, D.C.: U.S. Commission on Civil Rights.

———. 1983. A growing crisis: Disadvantaged women and their children. Clearinghouse publication no. 78. Washington, D.C.: U.S. Commission on Civil Rights.

U.S. Department of Labor, Bureau of Labor Statistics. 1984. Working women and public policy. Report no. 710. Prepared by Janet L. Norwood. Washington, D.C.: U.S. Department of Labor.

Vanek, Joann. 1978. Housewives as workers. In *Women working: Theories and facts in perspective,* edited by Ann H. Stromberg and Shirley Harkess, 392–414. Palo Alto, California: Mayfield.

Waite, Linda J., Larry E. Suter, and Richard L. Shortlidge, Jr. 1977. Changes in child care arrangements of working women from 1965 to 1971. *Social Sciences Quarterly* 58:302–311.

Waldman, Elizabeth. 1975. Children of working mothers. *Monthly Labor Review* (January):64–67.

Weitzman, Lenore J. 1985. *The divorce revolution: The unexpected social and economic consequences for women and children in America.* New York: The Free Press.

Yankelovich, Daniel. 1981. *New rules: Searching for self-fulfillment in a world turned upside down.* New York: Random House.

Youngblood, Stewart A., and Kimberly Chambers-Cook. 1984. Child care assistance can improve employee attitudes and behavior. *Personnel Administrator* (February):45, 93–95.

Zeitlin, June H., and Nancy Duff Campbell. 1982. Availability of child care for low-income families: Strategies to address the impact of the Economic Recovery Tax Act of 1981 and the Omnibus Budget Reconciliation Act of 1981. *Clearinghouse Review* 16, 4 (August/September):285–313.

Zelditch, Morris, Jr. 1960. Role differentiation in the nuclear family: A comparative study. In *A modern introduction to the family,* edited by Norman W. Bell and Ezra F. Vogel, 329–338. Glencoe, Illinois: The Free Press.

Zigler, Edward F., and Edmund W. Gordon, eds. 1982. *Day care: Scientific and social policy issues.* Boston: Auburn House.

Index

Magid, Renee Y., 91, 92, 105, 124
Marxist-feminist theory, and child care, 5
maternal deprivation, 23-24
maternal instinct, 24-25
maternity/parental leave, 87-88
men, and child care advocacy, 135, 137
Minnesota Mining and Manufacturing (3M), 77
Mondale, Senator Walter, 56-57
morale in companies, child care and, 111-12, 115, 117, 119, 122-24, 125
motherhood mandate, 21, 57
mothering, 6-7
mothers' pensions, 37
motivations for employer-supported child care, 103-28; absenteeism and turnover, 117-21; employee demand, 125-28; public relations, 124-25; recruitment and retention, 105-17; social responsibility, 121-24
multisite companies, child care by, 76, 132-33

National Conference on Day Care for Children, 53
National Employer Supported Child Care Project (NEESCP), 65, 66, 117, 120
National Federation of Day Nurseries, 35
needs assessment survey, 108, 109, 114, 127, 130, 131, 133
networks, of family day care homes, 71-73, 74
Nixon, President Richard M., veto of the Comprehensive Child Development Act, 56-57
non-interventionism, 26-27

nursery school, 34, 38-39
nursing shortage, 105-10, 138n1

Office of War Information (OWI), 47-51

parent education, 77-78
Parsons, Talcott (and Robert Bales), 4, 21-22
part-time work, 86-87, 88
patterns of use. *See* supply
Perry, Kathryn S., 91, 98n1
Philip Crosby Associates, 114, 115, 118
Polaroid Corporation, 80
Polatnick, Margaret, 24
privatism, of the family, 26-27
privatization, of child care, 59-60
Procter and Gamble, 82, 84
proprietary programs, 79-80
psychoanalytic theory, and child care, 6-7, 25
public relations, employee-supported child care and, 124-25

quality, of child care, 19-20, 146-47

Reagan, President Ronald, 58, 59, 60
recruitment and retention, 95, 105-17; effects of child care on, 115-17, 123-24
relative care, 17
role allocation, 4, 21-22
Roosevelt, President Franklin, 39
Roosevelt, President Theodore, 36
salary reduction plan, 82-83
San Francisco, Downtown Plan, 150n2
Scarr, Sandra, 20

About the Author

Judith Auerbach received her Ph.D. in sociology from the University of California at Berkeley in 1986. She has taught courses on family, gender, and research methods at Berkeley, Widener University (Pennsylvania), and, currently, UCLA. Her research interests continue to revolve around the intersection of gender, family, and work, particularly with regard to the institution of child care. Professor Auerbach has spoken often and has consulted with organizations and businesses on employer-supported child care.